'Cael O'Donnell empowers his readers to take ownership of their own destiny. By tapping into his gift for storytelling, he navigates what it means to live a spiritual life in a manner that's doable, tangible and awe-inspiring. *Three Minutes with Spirit* is a masterful narrative that guides its readers towards their higher purpose and psychic potential. In just three short minutes a day, Cael gently guides you towards your true north.'

Natasha Weber, @astrotash, resident astrologer for news.com.au, *Body+Soul* and *Mamamia*

'*Three Minutes with Spirit* is the perfect starter kit for embarking on your spiritual path. Filled with relatable and heartwarming anecdotes, deep wisdom and practical exercises, it'll take you on a journey to rediscovering yourself, understanding the deeper meaning of life and exploring the spirit world. Cael has a gift of explaining complex spiritual ideas in an easy and understandable way, making spirituality accessible to everyone.'

George Lizos, psychic healer and bestselling author of *Protect Your Light*

'Having connected with Cael recently, I'm in awe of his work. Everything he represents is inside this book, not to mention all the questions around spirituality that a lot of people need a   ing us with this magic.'

                              er, author and spiritual coach

'*Three Minutes with Spirit* is such a helpful and fascinating book. Cael has a brilliant way of introducing complex subjects like higher self, vibrations and Source and making it interesting to dive in and understand yourself better through the quick yet powerful exercises in the book.'

Camilla Sacre-Dallerup, bestselling author
and hypnotherapist

'The ultimate book for anyone on a spiritual journey! Cael shares his story in a relatable and heartwarming way, whilst giving readers tools to communicate with spirit in their own magical way. Easy to read, whilst evoking deeper ways of thinking and inspiring you to see spirit's magic is always with you in every moment of your daily life. Cael is an industry leader and seeing him generously share his gift in this way is truly inspiring for all.'

Janelle Bridge, psychic medium mentor

Three Minutes
with Spirit

Three Minutes with Spirit

CAEL O'DONNELL

EBURY
PRESS

EBURY PRESS

UK | USA | Canada | Ireland | Australia
India | New Zealand | South Africa | China

Ebury is part of the Penguin Random House group of companies whose addresses can be found at global.penguinrandomhouse.com

Penguin
Random House
Australia

First published by Ebury in 2022
Copyright © Cael O'Donnell 2022
Illustrations copyright © Zoë Zahava 2022

Cover photograph by Sarah Hyland
Cover design by Alissa Dinallo
Illustrations by Zoë Zahava
Typeset in 12.5/17 pt Fairfield LT by Post Pre-press, Brisbane

Printed and bound in Australia by Griffin Press, part of Ovato, an accredited ISO AS/NZS 14001 Environmental Management Systems printer

A catalogue record for this book is available from the National Library of Australia

ISBN 978 1 76104 668 1

penguin.com.au

MIX
Paper from
responsible sources
FSC® C009448

We at Penguin Random House Australia acknowledge that Aboriginal and Torres Strait Islander peoples are the Traditional Custodians and the first storytellers of the lands on which we live and work. We honour Aboriginal and Torres Strait Islander peoples' continuous connection to Country, waters, skies and communities. We celebrate Aboriginal and Torres Strait Islander stories, traditions and living cultures; and we pay our respects to Elders past and present.

Contents

Introduction

Everyone is different. We all have different worldviews, beliefs and backgrounds, and have been raised in vastly different ways. Some of us have secular views, others have deeply religious views; some of us love to daydream, others prefer to stick to scientific enquiry. However, there comes a point in most people's lives where we find ourselves wondering if something exists beyond what we can see around us.

Perhaps the same old answers you've been telling yourself your whole life aren't satisfying enough anymore, or you've had a recent personal experience that you don't know how to explain. Perhaps you've been curious enough to have already dabbled in spirituality, maybe even pursue some kind of way to make contact with the spirit realm. Perhaps you simply feel the desire to answer what has been calling out to you. In this busy world, it can at times be difficult to block out the background noise and listen to that niggling voice. However, you're likely here because you have a hunger for more.

Three Minutes with Spirit is for people at 'first base' in their spiritual journey – those who are interested in learning about spirituality but don't know where to begin. You might have seen me on TikTok or attended one of my live shows and are curious to learn more about my work.

I became a professional psychic medium a few years ago, although I've been communicating with the spiritual world since I was a teenager. My background is in mental health and therapy, but shortly after realising that my true vocation was helping people through connecting them with the spiritual world around them, I decided to become a full-time medium. By joining me on this journey I hope you gain an expansive understanding of spirituality and the spirit world, and learn how to zoom out from the conventional, linear view of Spirit that some of us have. There is more to the spirit world than what we might think and therefore I want to go deeper than even simply exploring the spirits of those who have crossed over and remind you of the most important thing of all: your relationship with your own spirit. I want to show you that there is more than what might be superficially evident to us and that it has always been this way. An entire world exists outside us, and if we embrace it with our eyes open, we will be met with much love and connection.

Now more than ever, people are awakening to this new perspective, however the reality is that it's not new at all. A lot of what I share in this book is reflected in many cultures around the world, which have held these views about Spirit long before mainstream religions took hold of the narrative.

This book is for the weathered soul who needs a reminder that your spirit is alive and well and you are not alone, despite the many challenges in life that have come your way. This book is also for the logical thinkers who want things explained without too much 'woo-woo talk' that can befuddle you before you even begin your journey. And finally, this book is for the heart-driven soul that seeks deeper connection to their loved ones in Spirit but also longs for a fruitful connection to Spirit in its other forms.

I hope this book will also provide a deeper dive for the curious reader wanting a place to begin with Spirit that isn't tied to a particular religion or practice but that instead is a universal exploration of how our lives can be motivated by the works and encounters of Spirit. There is no right or wrong, no definitive path that you must follow, no ideology you need to subscribe to in order to find community or to find yourself.

What is available to you that is soul-enriching, practically helpful, emotionally uplifting and spiritually comforting to evoke into your life? Perhaps you're a recent empty-nester and your identity seems to have shifted significantly, or you're a busy wife, mother and corporate climber who needs clarity on how Spirit is influencing your life. Or you could be a young person, highly aware of your own spiritual reality and wanting to seek out what is gently seeking you. The best thing about Spirit is that at a fundamental level it doesn't need to come knocking at your door; it doesn't need to threaten or alarm you to keep you involved. Spirit is an ancient force that will carry on perfectly well without your belief or awareness. Of course, that which exists in Spirit is thrilled that you have picked up this book to see for yourself what is out there.

This book is not just about linking in with loved ones as Spirit, but also Spirit as a bigger concept. It's also about how we can enhance our time on this Earth by reconnecting to ourselves ('self') and also to the universe ('Source'). You can choose to spend a small amount of time – just three minutes each day or week – connecting with what is greater than you, and when you do, when you recognise this existence and experience it fully, you will find that your life feels more complete, precious and accounted for in a whole new way.

Glossary

For any newbies to the world of Spirit who are reading this, welcome! Here is a brief overview of phrases and terms used in the book that might be unfamiliar to you. They will all be explored over the coming chapters.

Automatic writing	A method of communication from the spirit world in which a spirit is believed to manipulate a person's writing implement to convey a message, or simply inspire the writer to communicate a message.

Higher self — The eternal, omnipotent, conscious and intelligent being who is one's real self.

Human assignment — A divinely guided lifetime in which a person will achieve one or several positive outcomes to advance the world.

Inner knowing — An unshakable conviction that a particular decision or path is the one worthy of action.

Intuitive vision — You might know this better as daydreaming! It's the practice of tapping into your higher self in order to visualise what dreams or goals you should be truly pursuing.

Karma — Most commonly known as a principle of Buddhist or Hindu spirituality, it can be encapsulated by the following: Do good and it will be returned to you. However, the same goes for doing bad.

Manifesting — The ability to call forth what is waiting into existence.

Glossary

Older self   A prior version of yourself that occurred in this current lifetime. For example, your high school self.

Oracle cards   Oracle cards are similar to tarot cards and can offer more detailed insight into messages conveyed by Spirit.

Ouija board   A board containing letters and numbers, used to connect with those in the spirit world.

Past self   A self that relates to a supposed past life that imposes solutions to problems from that past life.

Pendulum   Any weighted matter hung from a fixed point in order to let it swing back and forth or side to side, in order to convey a message from the spirit world.

Psychic medium   An intuitive person that can channel the souls of the departed.

Source   The highest energy, where all things find their power to live and have their being.

Spirit	Any form of high or low vibration. This term is a bit of a catch-all, and can be interchangeable to mean loved ones in spirit or Source, depending on the context.
Spirit number	A numerical sign from Spirit of profound importance or meaning.
Spirit team	The combination of different types of spirit guides who are watching over you at any given moment.
Spirit world	An immaterial dimension of realms where different forms of spirits or energies exist.

PART 1

Looking inside

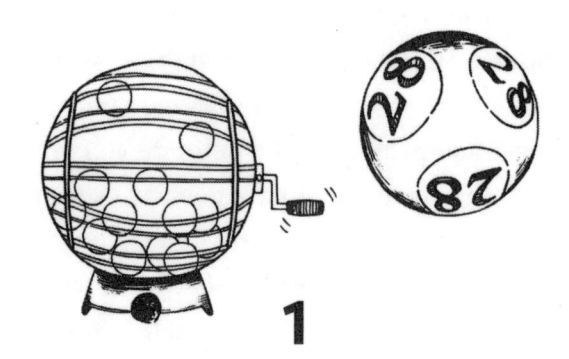

1

The probability of you

It's CLOSE TO A miracle in every sense of the word that you are holding this book in your hands. Why? Well, firstly, as my high school English teacher would point out, despite me failing all her classes, here I am with a finished piece of work! But it's actually because of the expansive improbability it took to get you here to the first page. I'm talking about the fact that it takes a long sequence of microprocesses mostly unseen by the human eye for a human life – *your* life – to become manifest in this world.

Did you know that, according to author and performance coach Dr Ali Binazir, the probability of you coming into existence is 1 in $10^{2,685,000}$? (And yes, that is a 10 multiplied to the power of 2,685,000!) In other words, it is practically nil.

Put it this way: the likelihood of you buying a lottery ticket tomorrow and winning the first-division prize worth millions of dollars is higher than that of you having come into being as the specific person you are. And yet here you are, reading this sentence with eyeballs that have evolved over millions of years to read a written language which itself took centuries to develop before being introduced to you by your parents or caregivers (most likely with some help from the furry characters of *Sesame Street*). The rich tapestry of human life on our planet is the outcome of more than 3.5 billion years of evolutionary history. Humankind has been shaped by incredible forces such as changes in the planet's crust, ice ages, huge fires and interaction among species. It continues to be shaped by these forces even now.

I know, my brain aches thinking about this stuff too – but it's so important to zoom out sometimes to see the beauty of what we call life. And not just our own lives but life across our entire universe. The conditions that it takes not only to bring forth life but also to sustain it are mind-boggling, and science has merely scratched the surface of it.

This is why we see human life as immeasurably valuable. We as a species are uniquely preoccupied with our own preservation. It's the reason we stop on the busy freeway to ensure that the woman in the car wreck is still alive; it's why we rush to the old man who tripped over on the footpath to help stand him back up; and, finally, it's why we mourn and grieve life when it eventually comes to an end.

But is it the end? Some of us are not satisfied with that abrupt, finite conclusion to life. Perhaps you have lost someone close to you, and have felt a greater knowing nestled somewhere within that says, *This is not all there is. It can't be. Surely this person who was such a significant part of my life can't have vanished altogether. We invested many years, meals, tears, joys, pains and countless other worthwhile things with them during their lifetime. How could this simply be all that I get with them?* Some of us feel compelled to search deeper to find the person who occupied what is now an empty space, a space once full of hugs, kisses, songs, laughter and other cherished memories.

This might be the very reason you decided to pick up this book over many others on the shelf: you somehow knew Spirit was calling out to you, wanting to deepen and rekindle your bonds to it.

An extraordinary cosmic dance

Isn't it amazing to think that in your one life you will only meet a certain amount of people? You physically won't be able to meet every person who is alive at the same time you are. In saying that, those who you do meet will have a great impact on you, leaving a memorable footprint etched into your soul and lasting love and admiration in your heart.

Take a moment to think of someone precious to you

whom you've lost. Now consider all the events and circum-stances that had to be aligned for you to have met in the first place. For a relative, you had to be born into the same family, within only a few generations of each other. For others, you had to be enrolled in the same school and had to have picked the same electives, or travelled on the same bus route, or been in the same workplace after having chosen to pursue similar careers, and so on. And you didn't go from stranger to friend overnight: you invested time, energy and many other resources into weaving together the meaningful relationship that you are reflecting on now that they are crossed over.

The entire elaborate process of meeting, bonding, growing, learning and enjoying all facets of our lives with those we love is a beautiful and extraordinary cosmic dance. We can't take for granted the little steps and larger catalysts at play that link us to other human beings every single day – especially to the ones who come to mean so much to us.

Some people will shrug off these links, labelling them as coincidences, nothing more than 'the circle of life'. But when we pause and take a moment to reflect, we gain a deep sense of reverence towards the personal connections we have made with our loved ones. Then, rather than letting the memories and bond gradually dwindle after their passing, we have the opportunity to stoke the fire that is still burning over our coals of kinship and love.

Letting go of old ways of thinking

When something happens in life that we can't explain, the temptation is to put a big red mental sticker on it that says 'too hard'. It can feel taxing to think beyond the surface, as if you are exercising a muscle that doesn't like to be worked. But I hope to show you that with a few small perspective shifts and a bit of practice, you can be linked to Spirit more than you have ever thought possible.

One of the first ways to do this is by stepping away from inflexible mindsets. That's thought patterns such as 'I already knew that', 'that's a funny coincidence', 'what a bizarre moment' or 'that is a weird phenomenon'. This is often the very language that Spirit is using to communicate with us; we just need to be open to listening to it rather than immediately dismissing it. You were born into a world primed and ready to teach you how to walk, how to talk, how to ask for food; the universe is constantly finding ways to connect with you and provide lessons, wisdom and comfort. You coming into this world with absolutely nothing is exactly how the universe needed you right there and then. However, sometimes it's how the universe needs us to be at other seasons too. When we open our minds and recognise Spirit, it will pop up in many unique ways.

But stepping out of these fixed mindsets is often easier said than done. For example, I attended a high school that offered philosophy as a subject to its younger students. I excelled greatly at it, and would fill notebook after note-book with thoughts that inspired or uplifted me. However, once I got to university to study mental health it became clear that to succeed in my degree I would be required to think analytically. As I delved deeper into the psychological sciences, I started to see the world from a linear and some-what dry perspective that took me into a depressed state of mind. Eventually, those notebooks full of thoughts that had meant so much to me in high school found their way into the bin. I had come to think of them as scribbles on a page and nothing worthy or substantial. At that point in my life, the world seemed to be a place with no purpose – a joyless and lonely place to be.

It took a lot of unlearning (and relearning) to shake off this fixed, analytical mindset after university and return to a more open, philosophical state of mind. But what kept me going was my belief that I was not alone. Even though I learned about many of the spiritual concepts I hold today practically on my own, I always knew that I was never alone. I could always feel the presence of Spirit guiding me – even before I knew to call it Spirit. You aren't made to meander through life with no support, help, guidance or direction.

An organising principle of Western society, where many of us live, is that we should fend for ourselves. From a young age we are taught to become unnecessarily, toxically inde-pendent. This principle shapes our world, our jobs, our

finances and our love lives. It also could be seen as a potential catalyst for ongoing mental illness, unemployment, and
homelessness. To move away from toxic independence can
feel scary, as if you're walking into the world with no plan.
This is when it's important to turn your requests to Spirit, to
ask not only for their support but to bring people who can
help into your life and your awareness.

Many non-Western cultures are not only extremely co-
operative and work as collectives, but they also understand
the concept that the universe never leaves us alone or forgets
us. How do they know this? They consider it within themselves to offer prayers and hold ceremonies that constantly
acknowledge their ancestors or deities. It's a daily ritual and
routine for them to constantly look beyond themselves for
strength and guidance.

As popular American author and organisational consultant
William Bridges said, 'Before people can begin something
new, they have to end what used to be and unlearn the old
way.' It's harder to unlearn existing things than it is to learn
new things, because of the brain's tendency to imprint and
maintain established ideas and thought patterns. But if we
can open our minds to possibilities beyond what we already
know and have experienced, and question some of the beliefs
we have unnecessarily clung to, we can create space to let in
Spirit and build a deeper connection to self.

There's no such thing as a coincidence

After conducting more than a thousand psychic medium appointments with people from all over the globe, I am the first to insist that there is no such thing as a coincidence. You see, our loved ones and spirit guides have the ability and capacity to manipulate our world from afar in such a way that gets us to stop and think. And while their actions may initially seem like coincidences or happenstance, I have seen enough from my work to know that this isn't the case. There is intention and meaning behind it all, and it is up to us to decide whether we want to look hard enough to find it.

Now and then a greater force comes into play, urging us to do something specific. Take the woman in the car wreck I mentioned earlier. Something 'out there' instilled in us the concern for human life that compelled us to take bold and risky action to rescue her. In circumstances like this, one improbability (her car accident) collides with another (us driving along the freeway at the same time that the accident occurred) to create an entire event that can easily be labelled a 'coincidence'.

Any time two humans are left to interact is an opportunity for Spirit to provide much-needed guidance, lessons, wisdom or comfort. We are often quick to forget that events in which we play even the smallest part can have a far-reaching impact on people's lives. It would be easy to dismiss the significance of your involvement in saving the woman from the car wreck by saying that anyone would have done it, or it's just basic human decency, but there's a reason you were in the right place at the right time. There's a lesson there for you too.

In the busy lives that we lead today, a lot of us aren't able to create time for spiritual connection. Often we are simply swept up and away into years (and sometimes decades) that disappear in the blink of an eye, all while our dearest loved ones are whispering messages to us that we miss because we aren't present or open to receiving them. But almost daily I am given reason to believe I am being lovingly surveilled by not only loved ones existing beyond me but also by Source and spirit guides that are calculating how to align perfect moments to bring forth even the smallest gains or change for me. And it's the same for you. It will likely go unnoticed by you directly but your spirit guides don't mind. As long as you are involved, the project will work.

It seems absurd to reflect upon the miraculousness of our own emergence into this world (remember how the probability was basically zero?), but then dismiss every event after that as some complicated equation of chance and circumstance and, without decoding it, toss it into the 'coincidence' bin.

I wonder how many 'bizarre moments' and 'weird phenomena' that have occurred in your life are piled up in your coincidence bin? If they were all closely examined, I'm sure you would be amazed to discover how many times it was actually Spirit or a loved one stepping briefly into your world to hold your attention for just a few seconds.

To understand Spirit, we must first understand ourselves

If we wish to connect to the realm of the Spirit, we need to begin by reflecting on ourselves. We play a vital role in the ongoing bond we have with those in the afterlife and it must start with us and our intentions. If you start with a chip on your shoulder, barge your way in and then shrink back into doubt, fear and uncertainty when nothing happens right away, that's not the gold-standard approach! But if your intentions are pure and you deeply want to connect into Spirit, it will gradually respond more and more. Often, Spirit will do its best to reach out, but it also has to be our responsibility to work with it and remember that we aren't the centre of this big world (although it's easy to slip into that thinking, given the success-based, egocentric society we live in).

Have you ever thought about how over time we humans have expedited processes such as boiling water to make them happen in mere seconds? Or how we have halved the cooking time of the traditional Sunday roast by using special ovens? We as a species are obsessed with doing things sharper and faster, and as a result, the average attention span today is only around eight to fifteen seconds. That's why platforms such as TikTok have boomed: people have less attention to give and need quicker gratification and higher dopamine dumps to their system than ever before.

But there is one process that has stood the test of time that nobody can speed up or slow down: gestation. Can you present to me a fully grown healthy baby in four months? No, you'd be crazy to promise that. What about a lazy baby that wants to be born after twelve months' gestation? Absolutely not.

This universe doesn't care about adapting to our fast-paced culture. Rather, each and every timestep in the universe is finely tuned. These are the domains in which our loved ones, spirit guides and Source move and have their being: in the dimension where nine months was set as the time of gestation on Earth for humans, the dimension that makes sure autumn, winter, spring and summer are spaced out correctly to ensure life-sustaining temperatures continue.

The dimensions that we often ignore or take for granted are the pockets of our mind that we will need to get a lot cosier with if we want to connect with Spirit or deepen our walk with it. Improbability made manifest is the universe's way of showing off. Your entire emergence is an example of the beauty that this universe is not prepared to slow down in producing. It's not a distant force that's indifferent to us. Just like the innate cry of a child when it is hungry or a dog's instinct to protect its owner, all these desires are highly calculated and placed there by Spirit – a higher force expressed through loved ones, Mother Nature and, of course, 'coincidences'.

The reason why you seek your loved one is because you're seeking a part of yourself. We see ourselves in animals because we are all Spirit; we connect deeply to art because it's an expression of Spirit; and we read books written by other human beings because they're an extension of the thoughts of Spirit. In every way, we are constantly and consistently taking steps to connect to this force.

So, are you ready to go deeper? Are you ready to link in with Spirit? It certainly wants to link in with you. Linking in with Spirit is not a massive commitment, nor is it an irrevocable commitment. Your curiosity about this book may not have been a coincidence after all – it could have been a gentle nudge from Spirit that will broaden and deepen this space for you and bring closure, peace and assurance to help you navigate the world.

Not only that, it's important to know why you are here in this world and who sent you. This is where we come to the higher self.

Three-minute exercise

List three 'coincidences' that have happened in your life (or that you know of); things you can't explain that seem miraculous. Then, start thinking about the other possibilities behind those events. Next, write down a few recent moments when you have felt connected to a higher force, and note how you felt in those moments – for example, peaceful, not alone, grounded.

2

A higher self

I WAS OBSESSED WITH all things circus as a kid and from a young age I wanted to work for Cirque du Soleil. Whereas some teens my age were fanatical about *Harry Potter*, Pokemon, *Friends* or *Seinfeld*, you'd find me ordering copies of the various Cirque du Soleil shows on DVD and watching them repeatedly to study the production efforts of each act and the mesmerising movements of the performers. I would spend hours on the weekend going through Cirque du Soleil memorabilia and watching behind-the-scenes interviews.

When you watch one of these magical productions, if you didn't stop to think about it, you could be forgiven for thinking that everything that occurs during the show is happening seamlessly all on its own. It looks so effortless that you become totally immersed.

However, there are voices the performers are listening to that you can't hear, namely the voice of the stage manager. Performers are being told when, where and what to do on a perfectly timed sequence that is organised by an amalgamation of subtle audio cues and lighting. Though the company is made up of a variety of former Olympic athletes, musicians, entertainers, performers and stage-hands who all speak a variety of different languages and dialects, the one language they all must know well is the language of the stage manager. Without the manager, the show would miss crucial timing prompts, performers would appear on stage when it wasn't their turn, dancers would be moving to the wrong music and ultimately, the whole show would fall apart due to severe mishaps and costly accidents.

The same goes for your life.

A stage manager is working in the metaphorical wings of your life right now. They are watching the show from a bird's-eye view and from many angles you are not privy to. They are cueing and inspiring various endeavours and evolutions month after month so that each one manifests at the perfect time.

This 'manager' is acknowledged in many cultures, spiritualities and religions and called many titles. It's often referred to as your 'soul' but in modern spirituality we have begun to call this the 'higher self'.

The presence of your higher self

The higher self is the stage manager in the wings of your life, assisting you by sending subtle prompts that can be felt in a variety of ways. The most common of these are gut instincts.

I'm sure you've heard the phrase 'trust your gut'. There is a truth to this and basically what it means is that it's best to trust the manager overseeing your life. Trust that they have a clear view from behind the scenes and are dropping intuitive feelings into your belly that tell you what to do and when to do it.

The higher self is also the thing that inspires you to take the high road in a given situation. For example, we've all been inconvenienced when we are commuting or even as a pedestrian when a distracted driver cuts us off at some point in our day. To decide to not react abruptly or angrily is to take the 'higher route'. This is another small example of the ways our higher self is interacting with us and nudging us along in our day-to-day lives. You can actually feel your higher self sometimes; it presents as a feeling hovering above your head.

Let me ask you this: how is it that sometimes you know things will happen before they occur? How do you realise you're aware of something that you never learned? Why do you feel a familiarity with seemingly random people and places? This is your spirit pulling historic data from your past lives and divine intuition (which I'll come back to in more detail later). It's a peculiar phenomenon but it's certainly one not to be worried about.

Your higher self is completely and totally aware of the current life mapped out for you, from start to finish. It knew the second you would be born and the events preceding it; it knew which parents you would have and even knew the hospital or place you would be born at.

Think of it this way: if life is a sailboat, your higher self is the rudder. It is steering your life. Although it's one of the smallest parts of the vessel, it is the thing that makes all the difference. The sailboat could be experiencing an impressive downwind of six-and-a-half knots in the most perfect patch of the ocean but if you don't have a rudder, you'll be going around and around in circles.

Though the higher self plays a vital role in your life, because it's always fully submerged in water it's usually unseen and unrecognised. But even though the higher self is buried deep in the waters of possibility, it is working tire-lessly, completely unfazed, and never inconvenienced by what is happening on the surface of your life.

The higher self is always conscious and listening to every conversation and every thought. It observes our lives through our eyes, remaining sensitive to any minor or major change and knowing the precise moment it should spark action.

The human assignment

Isn't it cool that we aren't all carbon copies of each other? Isn't it inspiring to know that we don't have to achieve the same things other people are achieving?

You would be surprised at just how evident the guidance from your higher self is in your life. Even if you are oblivious to it, your spirit is truly aware of what it's doing here on Earth. Consider the following: Why did you want to go into paediatric nursing and not pro wrestling? Why did you want to be a copyright lawyer and not a helicopter pilot? Why did you want to pursue event marketing and not biochemical engineering? What was the lynchpin factor that decided the outcome? It was your higher self.

See, your higher self knows exactly where you're going and exactly why you are here. Even at those times when you feel adrift, lost at sea, have faith that your spirit guide is working away, just below the surface, to steer you back on course.

Every facet of your life – from the romantic partners you might have, the careers you might pursue and the children you might someday raise – is all known to Spirit. All of these pursuits are stepping stones leading you to a larger and more determined assignment. This assignment is a special project that's looked upon favourably by the spirit world, and it is none other than the human assignment. Your higher self needs your humanness to bring about its perfect plan. Your humanness gives your higher self its most powerful leverage: permission to be on the Earth. See, any spirit that wants to interact on the earth plane and make the biggest impact must meet one simple prerequisite: it needs a physical body to inhabit. And that's exactly what your higher self decided to do before you were born: pick a body to enter Earth and complete *one* assignment.

Without our bodies, we are a perfect or complete spirit but the moment we enter the physical body we enter into humanness. This condition can be a blessing but also a curse at times. Just as we need humanness to enter Earth, humanness can be the biggest distractor in our life. Humanness can get us caught up in addictions, toxic relationships, unhelpful patterns, stagnant ambition and so on. Those are the obvious distractions; some are less obvious, such as feeling locked into the paradigm that you have to climb the corporate ladder, hustling for more and more money and desiring recognition and glory purely for your own sake. We can be easily distracted from the assignment laid out for us, that we ourselves chose before we were born, but the positive news is, even a minor distraction can be turned around for good by your higher self and used as a tool for growth.

Sometimes it takes defining what is *not* our path to truly figure out what *is* our path. Take me as an example. Given my intense love of the circus, my ultimate childhood dream was to work as a stage manager at Cirque du Soleil, cueing performers, animatronics, pyrotechnics and choreography. Once I got to the end of my senior year of high school, however, it became apparent that this path wasn't viable for me. I had not attended a single circus school class and relocating from Australia, where I lived, to Canada, where Cirque du Soleil is headquartered, was not on the table. Looking back now, although I still love the world of creative arts and performance and probably always will, I know why a whisper in my head made it clear that my Cirque du Soleil ambition was only a dream and not my true path.

Instead, I studied mental health and rose quite successfully to work as a therapist and mental health professional. I was recognised for my advanced skills in working with people from a range of backgrounds who were grappling with trauma and behavioural challenges. Whereas some senior people in my industry were content to stay in the same role, seemingly oblivious to the next rungs on the ladder, I was set on going all the way!

At one point I was working in a specialised team in the local hospital's mental health unit. It was a job that came with high stress but also a strong feeling of satisfaction, as I was helping patients with suicidality. Initially I felt compelled to climb the ladder in my field all the way to the top in order to best help people, but the further up I went, the more miserable, constrained and lacking in purpose I felt. I wasn't on the totally wrong track but I certainly felt that I'd hit a ceiling in that profession.

Around the same time I started to become aware of something quietly whispering to me about my gift as a psychic medium. I had discovered this gift in my adolescent years, when I would predict engagements, birth announcements and even relationship break-ups. Nothing was much of a surprise to me. I liken my psychic gift to when you watch an old favourite movie. You have seen it so many times that you know the protagonists, the plot and the ending. For much of my life, my gift has allowed me to glimpse things – not for any old reason, but so that I would be prepared. Prepared to be the shoulder to cry on for my friends; ready to adjust to changes when my sister fell pregnant at fifteen years old. Being attuned to my gift early on allowed me to live proactively as opposed to working reactively.

But while I was focusing on my career, I pushed those niggling feelings away. *I could really take this to private practice and open my own clinic*, I remember thinking to myself. I had many thoughts in that vein but something inside was no longer interested in helping people in a clinical, corporate environment. I knew I had to go much deeper and further. With hindsight, I can see I was being nudged by my higher self to use my gift as a medium to help others.

You see, ever since I was young I had pictured myself standing in front of audiences and speaking to them (maybe that explains my obsession with the circus!). I would stand in our big front yard and practise announcing and public speaking with an imaginary microphone, or even a repurposed stick. One of my most formative thoughts was that I would one day speak in front of rooms full of people. I had a sense that I would become known and that I would make a big impact. Your human assignment is often whispered to you in your formative years. That means that even from a young age, you've probably had an inkling as to why you were here on the Earth. My higher self was using its ability to cue self-reflection in me so that I would look back on my childhood aspirations, re-evaluate my life as a therapist and ask myself if I was happy.

When you've allowed things you truly want to flow into your life, you'll find that happiness comes easily. When you are aligned with your higher purpose, a pervading feeling of contentment and pleasure will hold you like a foundation in any given season.

Some people are existing right now in expired seasons. They might be experiencing worn-out feelings of dissat-isfaction – a tell-tale sign, but one that they're slow to acknowledge. An expired season isn't so much a financial issue as it is a time issue: the time spent walking around in the wilderness of one season can borrow time from future seasons. Ask any director of a Cirque du Soleil show and they will tell you that if a performer trips mid-sequence and they have to quickly dim the lights to allow them to get off stage, it sets the entire show behind a fraction of a minute and that is a time-costly error.

It doesn't matter how long it takes or how many avenues you walk, if you are in an expired season, Spirit will find a way to wave a flag that says 'move on'. The reason we sober up to the fact that we are in expired seasons or realise we are grossly unhappy is usually a nudge from our higher self to thrust us forward to our 'higher assignment'.

Some people's higher assignments are quite public, such as those of Martin Luther King, Mother Teresa and Oprah, whereas other assignments are 'subtly impactful'. Most of us will have a subtly impactful time here on Earth, but in no way should this be discounted or seen as 'less than'. I call these lives 'blessings in disguise'. There is no way to measure the amount of times your life has been perfectly positioned to be a 'blessing in disguise' to an unsuspecting person. Perhaps you said something at exactly the right moment or you offered help in someone else's hour of desperation. Perhaps you set an inspiring example for someone else to follow without realising it. All of these things are arising from the higher self, giving us an inner stirring that prompts us to take a step in the right direction. And the more we are living in alignment with our higher self, the better impact we can make in the time we have.

The only mentor you need

For as long as I can remember, up until around the age of 22, I was always seeking external validation. I wanted to know that what I was doing was the 'right' thing to do. It first manifested in my appearance and how I dressed. I was always making sure that I kept my style aligned with the trends of the time, and wanted my cologne to be top-of-the-line. Not only that, but I went to the gym religiously and followed strict diets because I wanted to be seen as fit, attractive and desirable, and somewhat important. I did all of this because I felt I needed validation from other people to be remembered in this world.

I would also call upon life coaches and mentors, wise counsel and those who provided 'spiritual oversight' – I even went as far as befriending an Anglican priest at one point. I never felt as though I could steer myself and truly lead my own authentic life. I linked all of this back to a childhood trauma where I was never trusted to make my own decisions and I was labelled as problematic and incapable. Thankfully, I have now outgrown those labels tenfold, but my lack of self-assurance really dominated back then.

Maybe you, too, have felt at times that you needed to 'seek permission' from the world to do X, Y or Z. But the truth of the matter is that you don't need other people's permission at all. They can be helpful and provide wonderful insight, but at the end of the day it all comes back to you.

Ultimately, our higher self is the only mentor we need. It is the number-one most reliable and credible source of clear insight, firm direction, guidance and support. This is because it is flawless by its nature; it is not tainted by humanness. If there's a dicey decision that you have to make or you're in the middle of an emotionally draining dispute, your higher self can stay calm and steady. As humans, our confidence waxes and wanes; it is unstable. We often overthink decisions and have to navigate other human relationships head-on, which can be taxing to our psyches and can constrain us if these stressors go unchecked. The higher self, on the other hand, is assured and has no second thoughts about the purpose you have in this lifetime. It is not judgemental or easily frustrated. It is using time wisely to bring about the bigger reasons you are here.

These 'bigger reasons' see no boundaries, borders or limits. They aren't affected by what country you live in, what language you speak, what culture you belong to or what your financial status is. Your higher self is not at all interested in any of that. See, you weren't just born to pay your taxes, take out a decades-long mortgage, find a committed partner or even start a family. Not even the illicit drug user or homeless person you passed on the street is existing without purpose. Most of us have found ourselves hitting rock bottom at some point, but we have to hit rock bottom in life to realise that our higher self, when all else is stripped away, remains our core, and our Spirit. You have everything you ever need inside of you; there is no other half on this Earth that you need to find. You can sit within a very precious peace when you radically accept that you are complete and enough – right here, right now.

A spirit being

Your higher self has you here on Earth for this specific assignment, which has a beginning, a middle and, of course, must have its end. We talked in the previous chapter about the breathtaking improbability of you entering Earth and manifesting a life here for a period. Now let's consider the other side of that coin: where do you go when the assignment is over?

I can say it in very simple terms for you: when we pass away, we merge back into the higher self. Imagine this as if you are taking off a costume or bodysuit and are revealed again as the true nature, the most authentic part of you: that is a living, flowing being outside of time and the realm of the physical. That is where you will return.

Let me put it this way: when you are alive you are a human that is *being* . . . when you are dead you are simply a spirit that is *being*. You begin as a spirit being, then become a human being that will one day become a spirit being once again. (Will your spirit ever return to be human again? It could, and we will explore this in Chapter 10.)

As a medium, when I am communicating with spirits that have crossed over, I am merely communicating with ex-humans that have returned to their higher self. I am talking to authentic, unabridged, untainted forms of being. A higher self is clear-minded. It doesn't contain the grossly limited capacity of a human mind that competes with evolutionary processes and psychological chemistry. The higher self could even be described as the 'complete mind' – the mind you wish you had all the time. The one that doesn't jump to conclusions, become paranoid, feel unworthy or feel depressed, or harbour resentment, jealousy or anxiety.

Some people's assignments go for a long time, others' are short and sweet. Others' are not so sweet. We might face tragedy, repeated trauma or crises that leave us feeling disempowered, hurt and afraid. These are seen as messes, and our higher self, along with Source, will make the most of the messes in our life. Your loved one in spirit experienced many messes too, but neither of you would be the same without having experienced them. In fact, they make up a big part of who you are in this lifetime and will teach you something very special that can never be taken away from you. As we'll see in the next chapter, our mess is actually our mirror.

Three-minute exercise

Find a quiet place, take some deep breaths, and try to tune in to your higher self. Can you hear it? What is it saying? Perhaps you can even start to feel it hovering above your head.

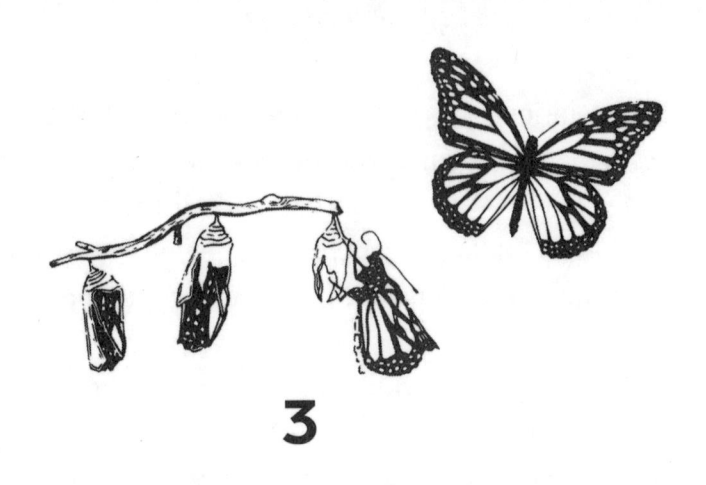

3

Our mess is our mirror

LIFE IS NEVER ALL smooth sailing. It can be much messier than we expect. But whatever setbacks you experience – no matter how life-changing or impactful – can be turned around and used to reflect your higher calling and purpose back to you. You see, your mess is a mirror as much as it is a miracle. Our mess is a reminder of where we have been and where we are not going back to ever again. It is a yardstick that can be used to gauge how far we've come. You might be thinking that your story, experience, trial or tribulation doesn't mean much, or that it feels insignificant to the world, but there's a wider purpose at play. Your mess, and that you were able to emerge from it like a butterfly from a cocoon, is a mirror.

While the caterpillar's metamorphosis into the majestic

butterfly may seem fantastic from the outside, this transformation looks gruesome deep inside the chrysalis. Did you know that for a caterpillar to turn into a butterfly, it must digest itself? Only then do sleeping cells awaken to grow the body parts of the future butterfly. And you thought puberty was mean!

Transformation is never easy or pretty, but it is the outcome that makes it worth the wait. Why? Because often it's not just you who benefits from your transformation. Have you ever pondered the fact that one of the most exciting and anticipated encounters on Earth is to witness or even catch a delicate butterfly? For some reason, no matter whether you're a fully grown adult or a young child, we all feel giddy and full of wonder when we see a butterfly. However, that newly fluttering butterfly will never in her life see her own wings. Although she went through the long and taxing transformation process and graduated with a beautiful set of wondrous wings that lift her off into flight, she will never know of or witness the true splendour that she is displaying to the world.

This is the same for you. The trials and tribulations we face are often cocoon moments that, although uncomfortable, dark and extremely lonesome at times, are actually growing us into something so glorious and magnificent that not even we ourselves will be able to witness the effect it will have on the world. You might be wondering why you attract some people more than others who seemingly want to hold on to you and constantly be around you. It's because they can't get enough of your splendour. Although perhaps unbeknownst to you, you are emitting an astounding energy.

Picking up new vibrations

Every person radiates what we call a frequency energy, or a 'vibe'. We all feel it, we all know it's there, just like catching a whiff of a woman's perfume on a still winter's night. Your frequency is a field of energy that you emit into a space. We can pick up on people's vibes non-verbally or even without seeing their facial expressions. People who are highly attuned to this will see, for example, a person at a party smiling and looking jovial but can still sense they are 'off'. This understanding that someone isn't feeling quite right comes from the in-built ability to pick up on people's vibes, frequency, energy or vibration – whatever you prefer to call it.

The miraculous thing about our vibe or energy is that it is unseen. It is something that we ourselves usually can't distinguish, but others will see, feel and pick up on it. And once we have endured trials and tribulations that we choose to rise from, our frequency or vibe is modified in a very positive way. It is revamped! After we've undergone our own messes we are given the prospect of being revealed as a new and developed version of ourselves, richer from the lessons we have learned, and those around us can sense the change in our energy.

Every challenge that we are able to survive and pass through – whether that's days spent suffering in hospital, periods of feeling depressed and helpless, or breakdowns of significant relationships – is not without purpose or meaning but instead comes with the chance for a 'spiritual upgrade'. It's a hope-giving idea that nothing we face in life, as hard as it might be, occurs simply for us to suffer or endure it. There is always something that will come out of it that will position us for our good; something we learned from that season will later in life become extremely valuable to implement, though the lesson may not be immediately obvious.

I once worked at a petrol station, and had a grumpy manager. He would often erupt into tantrums that were visually distressing. He would throw things, shout and simply become a dysregulated human for a good 30 minutes a day. However, I learned to hold my ground in those moments and stay humble, and this became the cornerstone of my work in acute mental health care. Each day that I walked home deflated by my tyrant boss brought me one step closer to being ready to handle the clients waiting for me in the psychiatric ward a few years down the track. Instead of looking at my employment at the petrol station as somewhere I would be lucky to escape from, I recognised it as a stepping stone and a training ground for me to be better positioned for future success. I would tell myself daily that no matter how messy the shift was or what mood my boss was in, one day I would work for myself, one day I would be my own boss, one day I would be happy and successful. Fast forward many years and here I am. I have a team of staff I treat nicely, and the best thing is, I work for myself and nobody can threaten to fire me for no good reason.

I choose to look at it like this: our misery will often open our destiny. When someone has been poor, they work hard so that they never have to be in that position again. When someone has hungered, they hustle like they've never hustled before so they will keep their stomach full. Our misery will unlock, spur on and push us to working out our destiny.

Whether our hardship took place yesterday, last year or seven years ago, we are the finished products of desolation. No one likes to endure these things when we are facing them – being the sentient creatures that we are, humans pursue pleasure and avoid pain. But the hope-giving prospect that lies before us is that, no matter the mess we have endured, if we stand today as survivors, we are nothing short of a living miracle, bearing and emitting an energy of strength and self-affirmation. And this newfound energy will undoubtedly attract new things to us.

My biggest mess

One of the biggest messes that has become a huge part of me is the reality that I am an adopted child. I can still remember it as if it were yesterday – hopping out of the fancy government car with that new car smell, being picked up into the arms of the social worker as my adoptive mother ran out into the front yard with both hands over her mouth, in tears and completely overjoyed by my arrival. After all the houses I'd arrived at previously, this one felt different. It felt like a home.

However, before my adoption I had been through the foster care system. Foster care life was messy. Especially for me at the time, as I was a toddler – barely two years old. Not knowing what was going on, who my real parents were and which house I belonged to made me a lost and confused young boy. I suppose 'messy' is an understatement in my case; it was a dreadful nightmare. I was often left without food on filthy sofas for hours, what teeth I could grow became rotten almost immediately due to the copious green cordial used as a supplement for real baby formula, and the sounds of glass smashing and shouting jaded my young soul as I was placed in the 'safest' foster homes that could be found.

The messiest moment happened when I was around two years old and my siblings and I were abruptly separated from each other into different permanent adoptive homes for the rest of our lives rather than staying together in one adoptive home. This shattered me from the inside.

You could only imagine the mess this does to a developing kid trying to find who their 'tribe' is. For many years I had no clue who my real family were. I had no idea about my Aboriginal culture either, nor did I realise who my siblings or birth parents were. The system had and still has flaws in the way it helps adopted children deal with the process of a new family.

Many years on, I'm thankful to have reconnected with my birth siblings and restarted the relationships with them that were halted in childhood. My siblings (and their offspring) reflect to me important truths about myself and also provide much-needed support. What was taken from me in my childhood waited for me and was returned in my adult years.

Consider the apple seed. You could leave an apple seed on your kitchen bench for fifteen years and it will never sprout and yield an apple. You could speak kindly to it every day encouraging it to grow, you could pray to a god, trust in manifesting, perform a ritual right in front of it – but it will never propagate a single branch and drop an apple into your fruit bowl.

That's because the apple seed needs the correct conditions to flourish and bear its fruit. And yet, when the apple seed is plunged into a cold, damp, dark patch of soil, seemingly left alone, abandoned, forgotten and useless, do you think for a moment that it believes that it is going into the correct environment? It would be thinking the absolute contrary. It sounds like a wretched place. But whoever placed it there did so for a very special purpose and knows exactly what awaits.

See, you might be feeling or have felt in the past like that apple seed in the ground. Perhaps for a long time you have felt as if you have been plunged into the same arduous conditions with little purpose or hope left to extract. However, none of us will grow on the metaphorical kitchen bench. We won't soar, exceed and excel if we aren't dropped into the soil of hardship first. As difficult and perplexing as it can be, our mess becomes our mirror when we zoom out to see the bigger picture of our life. When we see the opportunities that lie ahead of us.

If I had stayed bitter, stirred and traumatised by my childhood adoption, I would never have driven my way forward to where I am today. But thankfully I did not. I forgave and moved on. I did my healing journey and released the past. I used my mess to first become my mirror, then my miracle and finally it became my message. I used my adoption and the lessons learned for good.

It's all already within

The best thing is, just like the seed, you need very little to continue towards your destiny. People are constantly looking outside themselves in an attempt to secure their destiny. I thought that when I got my therapy degree, I would be set for life and happy, but that was far from the truth. Why? Because although I could find work, I found myself alone at a desk in a fluorescently lit office, feeling bored and unfulfilled. Whereas Australian culture had taught me that university would launch me directly into a secure job that would make me happy because I'd be making money, the reality I faced was starkly different. I even flirted with the idea of going back to the petrol station owned by the tyrant – that was how lost I felt.

Then, once I became a social media influencer and an international psychic medium, I thought, *Once I've hit 500k followers I'll be set for life*, but I've stared at the numbers ticking over for a few years now and have only felt very lonely in doing so. I've learned that increasing digits don't lead to any more happiness.

The key is in knowing that nothing that will make you is ever beyond you. Read that again. Nothing that exists beyond you will ever secure, move or bring forth your destiny. Everything that you need to thrive in this world already exists within you.

Every animal, creature, plant and being that exists is completely sufficient in itself to bring forth its purpose on the Earth. It has an inner coding, a radar and a sequence inside to tell it what it's doing here. You don't have to teach a cat to purr, a dog to bark, a bird to lay eggs and so forth. All of these processes and purposes will flourish beautifully on their own. So just think how much more you could achieve, as a highly developed being, if you listened to the guidance of nature and followed what comes naturally to you.

Merely existing proves that you are a lot more capable than you ever thought possible. You have probably never been told to celebrate the fact that you exist. Yes, there are birthdays, but when have we thought of a birthday as a day to celebrate that we are just a beautiful creature alive today? You don't owe anybody a reason to be here and nor do you have to feel inferior if you think your life is at a stalemate. The miracle you are waiting for is closer than you think, not because I say so but because it's made evident in the midst of mess.

You are a human being and not a human doing. It is more important to follow your inner compass than it is to ever copy or seek a path because others are seeking it too. You have everything coiled up inside you, ready to unfold at the right time, and it does not require much from you except to keep it moving. It's important to accept that change is inevitable and that nothing taken from or added to your life removes or increases your life's value. You are valuable for simply being.

Would you ever be able to tell me why you disliked purple and preferred green in the sequence of a rainbow? The existence of one colour does not negate the value of the other. Those two colours can co-exist and you might prefer one more than the other, but they both hold the same value.

I wish I'd learned all of this a lot sooner than I did. I live in a society impacted by toxic beliefs about how many followers I need to be more likeable, how much more cash I need to be happier, and how if I lost more weight I'd have a better chance at love. However, that is a mindset I define as valueless today. If anything, your mess is making you, your trial is teaching you, your hardship is helping you for one purpose alone, and that is to position you for greatness at exactly the right time. To turn your messes into mirrors by building character and constantly adapting your frequency and energy to amplify your being.

A butterfly will never see its wings, an apple tree will never taste its fruit and you will never see the full impact that you are having on Earth and what enormous purpose is still yet stored inside you. But that doesn't mean it's not there.

Three-minute exercise

Take a moment to pause and reflect on the messes that you've come out of. Think of the things that you've been able to (given the odds) turn around for the good simply because you decided to. When you do this practice and keep these findings at the forefront of your mind, you will find that more often than not, your mess is spurring your life into its full and complete destiny, one step at a time.

4

Connecting to older and higher selves

IN TIMES OF NEED, we tend to look externally for support – to the latest popular self-help book, to life coaches or friends and family, among other possibilities – but have you ever thought of first looking within yourself? We are more than just ourselves; we have a wealth of untapped wisdom and expertise right deep inside us that can be called forth at a moment's notice. This is what we call older selves that can minister to us in this day and age. There is also the higher self that helps us connect into our greatness to come.

The existence of older selves

Did you know that I was *this close* to obtaining a black belt in martial arts? I was seventeen years old and only one season away from starting my black belt training. But as I stared down the barrel of a long list of requirements and a daunting public demonstration, I gave in to my self-doubt and quit martial arts altogether.

Years later, however, at a time in my life when I was feeling cut off from my past and searching for a way forward, I remembered one of the patterns I'd learned from my training. In martial arts, a 'pattern' is a sequence of self-defence techniques you have to present in a sort of choreographed routine. It's kind of like an aggressive dance. I was shocked that I could remember the moves even though nearly a decade had passed!

This is because of what science refers to as muscle memory. It is a memory of a motor task that becomes locked into our physical system through repetition, so that we can recall it and perform it with little conscious thought, even without having done so for a long time. We have this very same ability within our selves – a version of a muscle memory mechanism that stores 'older selves'. You could say that when I remembered the pattern from ten years earlier, I was invoking an older self.

Inside of you is a storeroom of tucked-away older selves: troubled selves, strong selves, confident selves and so forth.

They have all played their role in seasons of the past and now they sit, decommissioned, in the museum of you. And, similarly to items in an actual museum, a lot of these selves are still intact and functional, they just don't serve a purpose in the current day, because we have adapted to newer ways of being or forgotten about them altogether. Perhaps you have amended these selves because in the current phase of your life you require fewer of the traits your prior self possessed. But they're never far away.

How can a separated couple, having been apart for many years, rediscover their love in just moments? The love is locked in their older selves. How can a person, having given up alcohol, slip straight back into drinking as if they had never stopped? The habit is locked in older selves. Or how can someone sabotage a new relationship by immediately falling back into bad patterns of behaviour? You guessed it: these are all conserved in older selves.

These older selves are shed year after year, season after season, just as a snake sheds its skin. These 'sheddings' will occur naturally and rarely with much effort. When your current 'self' has served its purpose, it treads down into the basement of your soul to be put up on the shelf.

It's important that you shed older selves because doing so makes room for new paradigms, habits, approaches to life and so on. Remember, a snake that cannot shed its skin will likely die. However, many people struggle to leave their older selves behind, and as a result are stalled and stunted within a self from the past. You might have met someone like this before – someone who acts as if they are much younger than they are. They might be in their forties but still behaving like a teenager. This is because an older part of themselves is likely taking the lead because their developing journey may have paused itself in one spot.

Connecting to your older selves

All of our experiences, memories and past moments are locked away in older selves we've left behind. The good news is that these older selves can be recommissioned to serve you when needed, so that you can start striding ahead in your earthly assignment. What we have experienced in the past can be relevant in the present, which is why drawing inspiration from older selves is so valuable. The wisdom you have accumulated over the years is hard-won, so don't keep it locked away in the past.

If you feel worn down by life's storms, you may want to draw from lessons stored in your older selves to help support you through today's challenges. This can work in many ways. For example, you might have always had an infinite reserve of patience when it comes to dealing with your kids, or even with life in general, but for some reason over time you've become irritable and easily bothered by the smallest things. Maybe you used to be a highly motivated morning person who would regularly hit the gym and eat wholesome healthy food but lately you've let yourself go and can't seem to find the 'on' switch again. Perhaps you used to be a visionary with big plans but for whatever reason you've been feeling flattened and demotivated and want to reignite your old spark. I've even heard of people drawing on their older selves to discover the flirtatious, funny and affectionate magic of their romantic relationship that has withered and stagnated after the honeymoon phase.

A small way you can utilise older selves is to think back to a time when you recall having demonstrated a favourable trait you wish to rediscover, such as patience, or a mindset you were able to cultivate, such as resilience. Remember, everything you need is already inside you.

Three-minute exercise

Spend three minutes now sitting with yourself and pinpointing an area in your life where you believe that inspiration from your older self could be extremely valuable. Pay careful attention to the first thing that pops into your head, as it is probably the most important. Write it down, along with any memories you have of possessing this old inspiration, ability, trait, mindset or whatever it is that you are looking to recall.

As you hold this thought in your mind, speak to yourself as if your older self is listening to every word. Speak to it like an old friend and tell it that over the next few days and weeks you want to tap back into that past inspiration, ability, trait or mindset and that it would be extremely valuable if you were able to do so. It might sound like this:

'To my older self who showed [insert desired ability, trait, mindset], I want to recommission these things into my life now. I'm excited that in a few weeks' time, these qualities will arise back in me naturally.'

As you speak these sentences out loud, close your eyes and visualise yourself at that exact time. What hairstyle did you have? How did you dress? Clearly picture your older self smiling at you and passing you a gift wrapped up in red with a white bow. That gift is what you asked for.

If you're wanting to get rid of habits that are currently unhelpful to you, rather than dismissing your older self that once struggled with these habits, simply call forth a part of yourself that knew restraint and limits, and that was fine without the substance or behaviour in question. You might have to think back to your childhood to do this, and that's absolutely fine. Something to note here is that it is more important to ask for what you *do* want rather than saying what you *don't* want. The universe is listening to your desires, ready to fulfil them. If you constantly talk about what you don't want, it might still be picked up as something you do want. (More on this concept in Chapter 9.)

Older selves aren't to be discounted or seen as inferior to your current self. You are where you are today *because* of those older selves. You stand on the strong shoulders of your courageous older selves. Support from older selves can provide an invaluable life lesson or comfort. Again, this goes back to the principle that energy is never created and energy never dies. Whatever you need from the past, you already have in the present. You don't have to grieve a past self, a past season or a forgotten way of life. Not a shred of your inspiring history is erased or left forgotten as you pave the way for your destiny. It is anywhere and everywhere carried inside you, and you can shift right back into it by simply acknowledging it and calling it back.

Hearing from your higher self

In life we wear many hats and have many different labels pinned on us, from boss to caregiver to partner. These roles are often bound by various expectations and attitudes.

Whereas in one role we might approach a situation in a particular way, when we switch hats that same approach may be unfavourable or inappropriate. The more hats we must assume, the more puzzling the dance of decisions becomes!

One of the most liberating realities, therefore, is that our higher self is far removed from an affixed label, role or identity. There is no identity found in the higher self; instead, the best definition for it is energy with no beginning and no end, totally free. Eckhart Tolle, a well-known spiritual teacher, describes our higher essence as timeless, formless and unconditioned consciousness. It is unrestrained by the genetic and environmental influences that make up human-ness. Whereas we as humans are like ripples on the surface of the ocean, Tolle explains, the higher self *is* the ocean.

So when we face perplexing circumstances and feel overwhelmed by demands to make decisions, in addition to calling upon the wisdom of our older selves, we can also shift our focus and intention to appealing to the higher self. We can do this confidently because our higher self is so obser-vant. Unlike our busy and preoccupied family and friends whose advice we might also seek, our higher self can see everything leading up to our current moment of need and is clued into what direction, guidance or instruction would be most beneficial.

We can hear from the higher self through a number of channels. The most popular ones to observe are inner knowing and intuitive vision.

Inner knowing

An inner knowing is an unshakable conviction that a particular pursuit, decision, choice or path is the one worthy of action. It is a deep feeling that, despite the opinions and input of others, only one option feels worthy of deep consideration. Inner knowing is characterised by a resolute, sensible and calm conclusion and is not manifested from fleeting, groundless emotion.

You might get glimpses of your higher self's input when you catch yourself saying things like 'I just knew this was the right thing to do' or 'I felt it in my heart of hearts'. I really like the phrasing of the 'heart of hearts' because it's a beautiful expression of the specific feeling you get when you are truly attuned to your inner knowing. Inner knowing from your higher self is seizing an opportunity to move overseas, for example, despite the many unknowns and uncertainties that such a relocation will entail. Your inner knowing will tell you that it's the right thing to do.

(On the flip side, your ego or humanness is more like when you arrive at the airport's security checkpoint. You know you don't deal narcotics; you know you have no concealed weapons; you've never lit a firecracker, let alone contemplated producing a bomb. But you can't help feeling a niggling sense of illegitimacy as you approach the intimidating officers.)

We can trust inner knowing; it's the manifestation of our pure ideas without all the surrounding noise of our minds.

Three-minute exercise

To tap into your inner knowing, ask your higher self out loud to reveal itself to you through resolute conviction about something – perhaps a specific decision you have to make. Make it time-specific and give your higher self at least five days to make things clear to you. Throughout this time, make an effort to check in with yourself about how you feel about the decision. This could be by spending three minutes a day writing in your journal. Ask yourself where you feel you're holding the decision. Your head? Your heart? Your gut? Do you feel that you should or should not do X, Y or Z? By the end of the five days, your higher self will have made every effort to show you which path to follow.

Remember, trusting your inner knowing takes time. But have faith that the spirit world in the form of your higher self is 100 per cent capable and present in your life. Over time, your trust in your higher self will expand and come to you more naturally.

Intuitive vision

Many exceptional things you have done in your life started

as intuitive vision. This subconscious phenomenon occurs all the time, and is more commonly known as daydreaming. Businesses are created in someone's mind on the commute home from the toil of a boring job. Brilliant works of art are thought up while someone sips coffee on the verandah.

While psychologists consider this to be our subconscious chatter in visual form, to me daydreaming is an effective way to witness our higher self speaking to us in real-time. Our big-picture earthly assignment is whispered to us in our formative years, but smaller-scale assignments are being communicated to us all the time. These could be something as simple as reupholstering your couch or milestones such as publishing a book, finishing that song, taking new headshots or applying for a business loan.

The higher self is unfazed by the various hats, roles and societal standings you currently possess; its focus is your future. For example, you could be waiting tables at a café and suddenly visualise yourself making your first sale at your new business. You might be pushing paper at your office job to the sound of keyboards tapping and the photocopier humming while visualising your sold-out comedy show tour. Your higher self can also show you other things that await you, such as real estate, new additions to the family, romantic partners, friendships and more.

Your higher self will find moments throughout your day to communicate these assignments to you via intuitive vision, and the more you become attuned to this mechanism of contact, the more it will occur. Intuitive vision is a conscious stream of visual inspiration and premonition, flicking you rough drafts of your future throughout the day.

It's easy to become more aware of intuitive vision by paying attention to your daydreams. Where is it that your mind wanders off to when given half the chance? Take notice, because these are the clues to your path ahead. Glimpses of your future and your potential are important to catch and spend time mulling over because they stir up consideration that leads to action. What is displayed as intuitive vision will always be *you* in a better position. You with a more fulfilling job; you with a healthier lifestyle; you surrounded by loved ones; you in a happy relationship. While you ponder these thoughts that have been ushered in by your higher self, recognise that you're receiving well-intentioned desires that will likely reposition or even springboard you to new heights.

If it weren't for your daydreams sending you cues for 'the next thing' in your life, you would never take action. How could you be inspired to act if it wasn't first a thought imagined in your mind? If I hadn't started daydreaming about leaving my comfortable career as a therapist, you would not be sitting here reading my book and discovering how to bring more spirituality into your life. When we refocus the lens of our attention inward to catch the messages from our higher self, we clue right in to our future. We clue in to what is not only possible but, with time and effort, is more than likely.

Everything in your life begins as a daydream; everything begins as an intuitive vision.

You are never alone

Isn't it hope-giving, isn't it life-altering, when you sit back and ponder how, thanks to your older and higher selves, you truly are never alone? If aspects of your past self are better than your present, you have now learned how to invoke the past. If you're stuck sizing up your future with very little inspiration, you've got someone to help you with that too. You in the past, you in the future and you right now are all existing together in this one moment as Spirit. When you deeply reflect and consider this reality, you will realise that this whole time you've not needed external forces and agents to get things done, feel empowered or find hope. If it's not a piece of you in the past, it's a piece of you in the future that you are invited to invoke and trust in day after day.

Your life as Spirit is exciting. Your future rests on the shoulders of your potential, which will forever outsmart, outperform and out-surprise you. As your potential flashes and twinkles before you in your daydreams, and appears as inner knowing in the pit of your stomach, remind yourself that it has one purpose. There is something in your bigger picture that the higher self insists you do before you leave the Earth.

So let's proceed as I share with you the epiphany that has most powerfully revolutionised the way I live my life. It is a concept that, when remembered at life's crossroads and brick walls, will bump you back onto the path of assurance. Your voyage here on Earth is so vitally important and your higher self knows this. That is why it is doing everything in its power to move you to do this one thing: die empty.

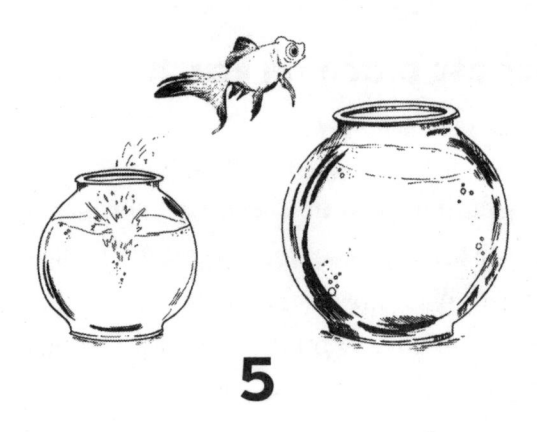

5

We must die empty

LIFE DOES NOT LAST forever; we all know this. And you've read enough of this book by this point to understand that our earthly mission, the one we have been put here specifically for, has already been determined for us, by us. How many years, months and days we are to be here to fulfil this mission has already also been decided. We can by all means love our life but we must also face up to the fact that one day our time here will come to an end. However, before we can leave this Earth, we must die empty.

The richest place on Earth

No matter where you're reading this, it's likely that somewhere near you – perhaps just up the street, perhaps a few suburbs away – there will be a quiet cemetery. This cemetery will be worth well over a trillion dollars. You might have thought the most valuable thing on the planet is the password to Jeff Bezos's bank account, but it isn't. It's this cemetery. *Cael, what do you mean?* you might be thinking. *Yes, there are some beautiful mausoleums, monuments and headstones out there that would be worth millions of dollars, but a* trillion? *Come on!* Well, I believe so. I'm convinced the cemetery is the richest place on Earth, and I'll tell you why.

What ends up buried there are all the books never written, songs never produced, businesses never started, inventions never built, movies never filmed, and other million-dollar ideas never brought to fruition. These are the desires, dreams, hopes, plans and ambitions of the dearly departed that never made it further than their daydreams. There is a worldwide pandemic of people dying without being emptied. They pass away taking with them all their uniquely individual gifts to a spirit world that has no use for them.

This concept was introduced to me when I was sixteen years old at a conference by the late Dr Myles Munroe. He was an inspiring motivational speaker who believed greatly in the purpose of humankind. His mission on Earth, he told us, was to give us the key to the kingdom, that kingdom being the rich tapestry of purpose and potential that exists inside us. I watched as he marched back and forth across the stage, beads of sweat glistening on his face, as he exclaimed to the audience, 'Die empty!'

His passionate words were profound and struck a chord within me that I can feel even to this day. But what did he mean? And why did this one concept never leave me?

Dr Munroe was referring to the idea of your higher purpose, which we've already touched on. As he put it, 'The value of life is not in its duration, but in its donation. You are not important because of how long you live, you are important because of how effectively you live.' We must do whatever we can to ensure that we do not let our gifts go to waste in the time that we have, but instead that we exhaust every drop of potential in us to live a full life that makes a difference.

For us to fully understand our spirit self, we must understand how important it is to totally surrender to our ambitions and dreams as they are dropped in, one by one, by our higher self. That is what our higher self is always trying to do: spur us on to find ourselves 100 per cent emptied before the grave.

At the conference that day it dawned on me that I didn't want to die and take my true purpose to the grave with me. This concept awakened a desire in me to be a continual light for others. I can honestly say that those two little words – 'die empty' – have changed the course of my life.

The Die Empty List

It's easier than you might think to understand the purpose of life according to your higher self. It has already been speaking to you for as long as you've been alive: 'Write a book', 'Start that business', 'Invest in that education', 'Pursue that dream'. In fact, I believe we reach out too far when it comes to trying to decipher our life's purpose, when usually it exists at the tip of our nose. It's right there! Your purpose has been whispering to you from seven o'clock this morning. It's been knocking at your door since last Thursday when inspiration struck but thanks to the humdrum moments of life, it vanished into the background and became another 'idea'. One by one, we tuck away these clues into our inner chamber and dismiss them with all kinds of excuses, like 'When I can afford it', 'When I've got the time' or 'When I've got my ducks in a row'. But doing this will never bring you closer to the purpose that your soul has here on Earth. You must attune to the inner agenda that is playing as background noise to your daily life and start putting it into action.

This is where my psychic work comes in. Many people still question their quiet inner agenda. They have a niggling feeling about the direction their life should go in but they need validation to feel confident that this is truly the path that they should take. They need someone to help them listen in more clearly to what their higher self is encouraging them to do.

What is it that your higher self is saying? Well, it's easy. I believe it was revealed to me from Spirit and the ancestors that each person has different things imprinted into the fabric of their lives. This is how I get my information as a psychic medium; all I'm doing is tapping into the map of your future and reading out what I'm seeing. That's why we call it a 'reading', because I'm reading to you the agenda of your higher self about the things that need to happen, the divine plan to empty you of your greatness. I like to call it the 'Die Empty List'.

A psychic medium can help you tap into your Die Empty List, or you can create one on your own by reflecting deeply on what you believe you are destined to achieve during your lifetime. Here is my advice on following the signs that will lead you there.

Look for the signs of expired seasons

'Argh, I have back-to-back readings today. Darn it!'

These were the very words of my industry friend, psychic medium Janelle Bridge. It was spring of 2021 and she had come to me feeling totally burnt out after seeing client after client. She wanted my guidance to understand if it was just a phase and she would shake this dead-end feeling or if she needed to think seriously about a bigger change. 'Don't you see?' I told her. 'That's Spirit emptying you and spurring you on to the next big thing!' She chuckled at the truth of my words.

You see, to help us perform the mission of emptying ourselves, our higher self will instil within us feelings of misplacement or incongruity. Maybe you've found yourself thinking something like 'I just don't want to work here anymore', 'This relationship is holding me back' or 'I know it's soon, but I want to have another child'. What if instead of bottling up and being in conflict with these desires, we allowed them to bloom to their fruition? They are signals that it is time to move on to the next chapter of your life. Perhaps it *is* time to quit that job and pursue a new one; maybe the relationship *has* dried up and run its course; or this *might* actually be the perfect moment to continue growing the family. These desires we often push away because they seem ill-timed and inappropriate often reveal a much larger purpose and chance for expansion. However, due to various factors, some being low self-esteem, fear of change or imposter syndrome, we recede into a terrible thing: stalemate.

Resist stalemate

I have seen numerous people in my life exist in a stalemate for years or even decades. You'll have seen some yourself too; they seem constantly put off by things and rubbed the wrong way, and smiles and enthusiasm are sorely lacking from them. When I got my first job at fourteen in retail, the same people that worked there on my orientation day were the same people that worked there when I came back ten years later. I'm not saying it's a bad thing for someone to hold the same job for a decade, not at all; but an issue does arise when they look miserable, weathered and their words are filled with grievances and grumbles down the aisles. If we persist in a situation that makes us unhappy without making any attempt to change things and move forward, that is a decision we are choosing to make. Stalemate, stasis and stagnation are not what the universe wishes for us.

Misery is not a mystery, it's a crucial message. A person living to their highest potential will face disappointment, heartache and despair but they will not wind up feeling irredeemable sadness. How can you be despondent if you are following your highest purpose? To me that is simply not possible. Yes, you'll grieve, fall into doubt and be irked by various things that are out of your control but when you are aligned with your purpose, misery never sticks around for long.

Many people go through the motions of life, their purposes buried and dormant, waiting for 'the right time'. In fact, 'the right time' is the moment you feel out of place, like a fish out of water, no longer happy, because that's the right time for the change that is going to propel you forwards.

Any feeling that you want to achieve *more* is undoubtedly coming from your higher self. It's the strongest message you can get and the most important message of all, telling you to take the leap to the next phase of life. If you're thinking *But Cael, I can't find my purpose* – my friend, it has been waiting inside you all this time. It has been whispering to you from the shadows and in your dreams at night with that inner knowing of 'I'm not happy anymore' or 'I'm ready for something greater'.

Three-minute exercise

Spend three minutes writing a list of things that you feel have expired in your life and that you don't feel aligned with anymore. It could be big things or smaller ones: you don't like your couch, your hairstyle, your career, the degree you're studying for. Reflect on this list. Start with one of the bigger-picture items you've written down – perhaps your career, which can take up a significant part of your life. Ask first if it is what you want to be doing or if you feel there is something greater, and go from there.

For many, the list accrued in this three-minute task will shave years off walking in the wilderness of stalemate and purposelessness. The short chat I had with my psychic friend is going to save her another valuable chapter or season of resenting doing face-to-face readings, and instead inspire her to create more opportunities to help people, which is her highest desire. How can you step into your next chapter?

Pay attention to your grievances

The other place where your higher calling is often hidden is in your highest grievance. The annoyance and imposition is actually an opportunity knocking at your front door, but sometimes it's easier to pretend it's simply the neighbours or someone with a petition and just stay on the couch.

There are opportunities we have all missed because we don't realise the connection between what is afflicting us and what is attracting us. But the good news is that we can break out of grievances and find ourselves attuning to the higher self a lot better. There's currently a big shift happening in the spiritual community around inter-personal relations – instead of sitting with how we feel a person has done us wrong, we can reflect and ask, 'What is that bringing up for me?' If we look closely at anything that brings out feelings of injustice or frustration, we can find hints regarding what truly matters to us. If it's 'Why do I feel I'm resenting my sister's success?', perhaps the greater message is, 'You can be there too, if you're prepared to put in the effort.' Or if it's 'Why do I envy people who are self-employed?', well, perhaps deep within that is the true direction that is calling for you but you haven't been brave enough to take the action towards it yet.

It's often been said that the thing that angers you the most is the thing that you're called to fix in this world. Whatever keeps you up at night is the very thing you're here to leave an impact on. It makes sense, because why do some people have more investment than others? Why are some people staunch activists while others do just enough? Because without the fire inside various activists we would have no movements, no change and no evolution as a society. Spirit moves upon us to make various activist movements by raising up unquenchable passion inside a few people. It only takes a few people to spread a message and then make epic change. Look at the rates of veganism. According to *Forbes* magazine, in the USA alone, the vegan movement has seen a 600 per cent uptake in people ascribing to the lifestyle and ethical view in the last decade. This was because a bunch of people concerned about the ethics of eating meat and about climate change decided to educate other people about this lifestyle and view. This movement was sparked to life out of a sense of injustice.

Grievances are strong indicators and messages from our higher self. They're like little taps on the shoulder to tell us, 'It's time to move on.' But I don't mean that if any small grievance arises, we should just drop everything and leave our marriages, jobs or other endeavours. I'm talking about unshakable moans that shroud our inner heart of hearts.

Three-minute exercise

Spend three minutes reflecting on your latest grievance in life. What has it brought up for you? How has it changed the direction your life is taking? Can you see the bigger picture?

Don't wait to be rescued

At the end of the day, your life does not need to be redeemed by anything or anyone, only from the risk of stalemate. The most urgent need for you is not to look for redemption outside of yourself but to find that you can wholeheartedly live from the depths of yourself and empty yourself of all your greatness and majesty. Some people wait and pray to various religious figures and deities asking for support, help and guidance to 'find' themselves and 'discover' their purpose. Many others say they are looking for their 'other half' in relationships and think they must wait to find them before truly living.

Remember: coiled up deeply inside of you is the first and last of everything about you. You are not a half-completed being; you are whole and have been ever since birth. You are filled to the brim with every potential that you will ever need in this life.

No one can add nor subtract from your innate greatness – not you or anyone else. Once you fully understand this one truth, the world will become far more open to you. You cannot add anything new to your greatness because you simply are. And you can't take away from it. No matter what scandal, mistake or problem you face; you remain seated in divine greatness.

But again, nobody is coming to save you or rescue you or tell you that you're more than capable of shifting into a new season. Nobody is responsible for letting you know that it's time to branch out and take your life to the next level. That's why it's so important to realise that the person who takes responsibility and leadership of emptying you before you meet the grave is your higher self.

We are stepping into a time where it is more important than ever before that we radically pursue our dreams because within those dreams are a series of helpful changes that are monumental to the evolution and ascension of our world. By following your deepest dreams, you might become someone whose legacy contributes to monumental changes to the big issues that we face, environmentally and societally.

So, my friend, let us deprive the grave of all its undeserved riches and glory. Imagine if all of us went to our graves fully and totally emptied, so that every book that needed to be written, ever song that needed to be sung, every business that needed to open and every poem that needed a reader found its place on a shelf, playlist, museum, street corner or library. This is where our human greatness is required to be. Not in the grave. We aren't meant to serve the grave our glory, wisdom and creativity. We aren't meant to bury possibilities and potential.

So, finally, let me implore you, while I have your attention for a small fraction of your life: please return one day to where we all came from having lived fully and died empty, unleashing every shred of your greatness here.

PART TWO

Looking around

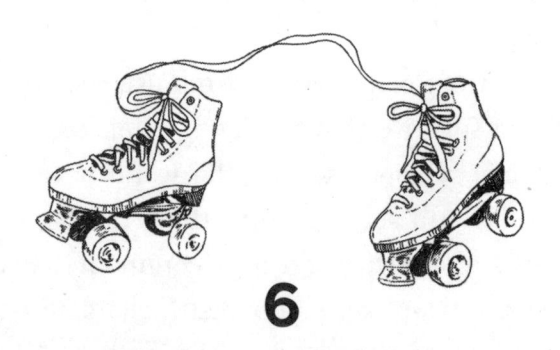

6

What is Source?

REMEMBER THE SAILBOAT FROM Chapter 2? I'm going to build on that a little here. Did you know that buying a sailboat can cost you roughly a minimum of $40,000? That is quite a lot of money, but if you are a dedicated sailor, I'm sure it is worth it. However, there is one thing that, until acquired, will render the $40,000 sailboat completely useless. This thing costs absolutely nothing – no subscriptions, no hidden costs or annual fees. It is free to the owner of the sailboat. It is wind power. If a sailboat doesn't receive wind power, it moves nowhere and is just a floating vessel of fibreglass.

If your life is the sailboat and its rudder is your higher self, Source is the wind in your sails. It gives us the power we need to embark upon our path when we are losing our way or need extra oomph.

Given its strong connotations of omniscience and omnipotence, it's no surprise that Source is often connected with religion. Some religions around the world have befriended Source, others still see it as something too big to comprehend. In the Western world it is commonly conceived as a force with humanlike, paternalistic characteristics, as is the case in the Abrahamic religions such as Christianity, Judaism and Islam. What better way to relate to Source than to impose on it traits that feel both protective and relatable but also authoritative and in charge? In other religions, Source possesses not human traits but animal traits, and in others, Source is something beyond us that we can't yet relate to in this dimension.

No matter its form, all of it is Source. Source is such a larger force beyond us that it actually doesn't require us to try to define it too strictly. It's there to guide you, to befriend you, to support you, to enlighten you and to lift you up. It can be whatever you want it to be.

Zooming out

For those of us raised to hold traditional views of monotheistic religions, it can be hard to unlearn what we have accepted our whole lives. This was my experience when I realised I didn't believe in Christianity and its particular God anymore. It was a life-changing experience because for a large portion of my life, I thought Christianity was the 'right way' to be attuned to Source. I thought I had found the truest religion and that I was in a relationship with this God. The penny didn't drop until I embarked on something so obvious yet so telling: I actually read the Bible properly. For years I had listened to preaching and had other people spoon-feed me this book, from parents to pastors to schoolteachers, but I never consumed it for myself. I just blindly believed it and went along with everyone else. Perhaps you have been in this position too?

What I discovered, no matter how many times I read it, was that all of the stories and inspirations, parables and lessons, have been around for thousands of years, popping up in many other religions and spiritual practices, from Hindu texts to African spirituality. Nothing in the Bible is new. All of it is just recycled knowledge from all the other spiritualities in the world. It made me realise that my concept of 'God' was very small and I needed to zoom out.

I had always felt second-rate with the God of the Bible. I felt dirty, naughty and like a black sheep of the 'Christian community' because I wasn't heterosexual. I felt that I had started off on the back foot with this God and was always pushing a rock up a hill to make him accept me. When I left Christianity, it was a logical thing to wonder: if God, as the most powerful being in the whole universe, truly hates non-heterosexual people, as it is written, why does he still make us in droves? Why are we still popping up all over the world, and even in the animal kingdom? And why does psychology declare that there is nothing that can be corrected about a person's sexuality, nor is it safe to try to alter it? That demonstrated to me that God was either absent, running things on autopilot and not aware that gay people were being made – or that a different God and Source exists altogether. As you could imagine, I decided to go with the latter. When I took that step back to see how Source truly manifests, I realised that there are thousands of beliefs and worldviews. There are even hundreds of worldviews and beliefs simply within Christianity.

Minutes v. millennia

Even though I knew I'd made the right choice in turning away from Christianity, I was still worried, scared and lost. I felt my whole religion was crumbling before my eyes and I had no back-up plan. I felt like I was dishonouring and de-converting and was turning my back on God and would be punished. It was so comforting to think I had found the 'true' God who operated as my Father, friend, shepherd and all those other great qualities. However, what I soon remembered was that I was sitting in a human body with Indigenous blood inside of me, fathoming that my ancestors had never heard about

Christianity or Catholicism until approximately 230 years ago. So what did my people actually believe? What was their Source? I had to find out. I decided to cleave to my Indigenous heritage and explore our beliefs.

I took a weekend getaway to Halls Gap, Victoria, a popular Australian tourist destination, where people flock in droves to climb the breathtaking peaks of the Grampians. On this trip I came across one of the most comprehensive and beautiful Indigenous museums, the Brambuk Cultural Centre, that tells the story of my people. At the cultural centre, the story of the Aboriginal people is told in chronological order on the walls of the tall building. The story begins at the bottom of a helical staircase and as you walk up the stairs and read the plaques you learn where the Aboriginal people first originated and emerged. As I climbed these stairs it never even dawned on me that I would walk down them not believing in the biblical God.

Once I had reached the top I had travelled back 65,000 years in time. I had learned of my ancestors' beliefs and struggles as they first discovered fire, and the stories they told themselves as to why thunder and lightning existed, and why some animals were dangerous and others were not. It was an elaborate explanation as to how First Nations peoples formulated their worldview and beliefs. And none of it had any stripe of Catholicism or Christianity. The straw that broke the camel's back for me was a statement on the display about how Christianity was forced upon my people only 'minutes' ago in comparison to the timeline of how long they had been around. We had believed in our own things for 65,000 years and had been doing great.

I walked down the ramp with many thoughts in my mind. I had realised that my culture was older than the religion I believed. About 2000 to 4000 years old is still a drop in the ocean compared to both the real age of the world and the emergence of my people. As I went through this logical and tedious process in my mind, many lightbulbs were going off.

We are all simply making sense of this world in our own ways. What can be experienced in Christianity is also being experienced in Hinduism; what good feelings are evident in Islam are also being found in a West African tribe believing in something totally different. What I realised is that Source is in all of us. This was revolutionary to my sense of self.

As the oldest culture in the world, I felt safe and validated in returning to the beliefs of my ancestors. I wasn't prepared to entirely discard the beliefs introduced to us minutes ago, but I understood how they were actually a product of someone else's culture and not my own. I believe we miss the point altogether when we try to believe in the 'right' religion or faith. Nobody is wholly correct, nobody is entirely right. What we are really desiring is to go deeper with Source and find ourselves moving towards a greater purpose.

The intricacy of this world, the improbability of life . . . how could it be a mistake? I believe that Source – or God, if you will – actually absolutely adores all humankind.

Source is both feminine and masculine and therefore has no gender or gendered pronoun. It is a foundational force that flows as the entire universe itself. It manifests in all that is. I believe it has no judgement, favourites or strict rules. I believe it allows us to learn with the forces it generates, like that which is observed in Buddhism with the laws of karma. I believe at the root of its intention is true and divine love that will never separate from a person. That is the one thing I can appreciate about my experience in Abrahamic religion: they get the love part kind of right; that everybody is loved by something greater. But then it contradicts itself by saying that there are conditions for this love. You need to be a specific sexuality to be eternally loved, you need to act a certain way and achieve a certain set of lifestyle goals. These are determinants of whether you'll be locked into the force of this God's 'great' love. However, none of those things are necessary. I am convinced that a person does not emerge without ongoing and persistent love adorning them. They are the object of a loving force beyond us that can manifest itself in many ways.

Source is . . .

. . . subtle

Within Christianity, I found 'God' to be invoked when and where he was needed, at the wave of a pastor's hand or when the books were opened. I experienced a lot of things theatrically in church that made it feel more like a rock concert than a holy moment. I believe that the ultimate knowledge of Source tells us that God is subtler than what we find in these religions. I believe that Source appears in the arms of a friend who supports you, the perfect timing of a need that has been fulfilled, or even in the moments where you pick yourself up and don't know how you were able to do it. I believe that Source does not exist stationary and seated in the apparition of a human body on a heavenly throne. I believe our God does not require a throne and is seated at the table of the poor, where they are abundantly provided for. God is found in the smallest acts of the everyday. You don't have to recognise Source for it to be there.

... self-sufficient

Source doesn't require worship, adoration, fasting, prayer or anything that places heavy burdens on the human mind or will. Source is simply there. Source is self-sufficient. That means that it doesn't need adoration, worship or praise from human beings. It goes without saying then that Source isn't jealous of you not going to church or listening to your own style of music, because Source is the frequency inside the music you like. Source isn't found in only eating vegetables and waking up very early to pray; Source is found right here in the very present moments of life. Some believe we wait until the end to meet Source, not realising that we have had it alongside us every day. It doesn't require anything at all outside of itself.

... there when you need it

There is already enough that is against us in the world when we arrive. One thing that will never be against you is Source. Because you are an extension of Source itself, you can never be rejected or removed from it. Source is willing to work with you if you can work with it. It's not your master or your guru, it's not your saviour or your parent. It can simply be seen as a friend. If you work closely with Source you will find your life can drastically change. When you break out of envisioning Source to be this faraway white man stalking you day in and day out, you will begin to shift the way life can flow through you. You are completely capable.

Take, for example, a rollerskating rink. As everyone is skating around the rink, some people are staying close to the rails, others are swishing and swivelling around. Still others are landing completely on their backsides. Source can be seen as the rollerskating rink itself. It doesn't judge you, it doesn't really care if you speak to it, it doesn't care if you are young or old. It will still be able to hold you. Also, the same consequences exist for all participants: if you don't know how to skate or if you are careless – and this will be all of us at some point or other – you will fall and injure yourself. But it's important to remember that the ground won't swallow you whole if you fall over, and your injuries will heal. The key is accepting that if you don't learn how to balance or master new techniques you'll continue to fall and injure yourself. It's up to you how you play the game.

Right now, you are skating around the rink that is the universe and there is no right or wrong way to do it. There is no right or wrong way to enjoy your time. If you want to move skilfully and elegantly, like you're doing a choreographed dance, there is that option; if you want to whisk through life figuring it out yourself, falling every so often but able to get back up, there's that option also. You aren't seen as needing to be parented by the rollerskating rink, you simply need time to learn your own way in your own time.

... liberating

Nobody is in charge of anybody but themselves. Nobody owns or controls you except you. This was another thing I could never digest as a Christian. You are taught that you are a slave to God and must serve him. This is a detestable image. It rings true to our dark past in certain cultures and the way the message of Christianity was spread not with hugs of love but with much bloodshed. Slavery is just a simple fact of life in the Bible. Source, however, sees you as a free roaming spirit. You aren't a slave to any being. You aren't a slave to your past or your future. You in spirit form are free completely to live your life on your own terms.

This might be a sobering and liberating message for some of you because you've been mollycoddled when really you never wanted to be. You've allowed something else – whether that is partners, friends, parents or religion – to tell you that your life is supposed to be lived a certain way. It's an uneven and unequal relationship that leaves a lot of us dependent and stagnant because we aren't able to mature and realise that the universe is not set up that way. You don't have to pray to a god and ask it to give you what you want. You are not dependent on anything or anyone in the spirit world. You are a capable and powerful spirit all on your own and you can manifest and bring things into your life completely on your own.

. . . already within you

This is the key. You might spend a lot of time looking outside of you but it's important to return to this concept I keep touching on. *You* are the creator, *you* are Source, *you* are this god that you pray to. You are the activator of your dreams, the arbiter of your future. You aren't separate from the universe, God or Source. A lot of us sit and pray to something we think is existing 'up there' when really our Source inside of us is listening to what we need or want, and then activating what it takes to get us there. You are the answer to your own prayers.

I don't mean to discount anyone's beliefs, but we don't have to ask Santa our whole lives for the basics of what we deserve and need. We can go out there and work hard for them and bring them home ourselves. We can manifest and bring things into our life that 100 prayers could never accomplish. You are the source of your desires and the keeper of your future.

When you explore this world, you may end up dipping your toe into many different belief systems about God, Source, religion, etc. However, the take-home message is this: we are all but one force and nothing is separate. We are part of this one universe and that is evident among all beliefs, tribes and faiths. We are all arising and being reminded of how powerful we truly are. We are loosening the shackles of the oppressive movements and systems of our past and seeing that, when the ancient dust settles, as people we are one and we find Source simply in *being* one.

However, we aren't left to simply live by finding Source and linking in with it. We are also here to learn, and to give and take from what we have and what we need. The next chapter will focus on this.

Three-minute exercise

Use three minutes to reflect on a moment when you realised that a higher power was operating in your life.

7

Learn and teach, give and take

WHEN I WAS FOURTEEN years old, I had a best friend named Ella. I loved spending time with her – we would make baked goods, meander around her garden and simply enjoy the small and mindful moments of life. Every Sunday after church, when the other kids wanted to go over to their friends' houses to play cricket and have a barbecue, I would ask my parents if I could go to Ella's.

'But why? Aren't you bored?' was the usual response from my family. 'What do you even talk about to an 80-year-old?'

I met Ella when I was twelve. She watched me grow from a child to an adolescent and would go on to see me grow into a young adult. Ella was a kind and humble lady who was often misunderstood. If you didn't know her well you might think that she was a miserable widow with only pessimism and negativity to share. This was because she often would complain about her life, and how sad it felt at times, as a way to open a conversation. Once you got past the initial feelings she harboured, you would arrive at a plethora of great topics to discuss. Not many people had broken through this barrier, though. I would often observe people speaking to Ella in a condescending way, as if she were too old to understand them properly, but they could not have been further from the truth.

Ella and I had a strong bond that nobody else understood. I feel that Ella opened up to me because she realised I had the time and the attention to listen to her. We were capable of talking with each other freely about absolutely anything. Ella used to be quizzed by others as well. 'What do you and Cael even talk about?' I overheard someone ask her one day at church. Ella responded, in her usual matter-of-fact tone, 'Oh, anything, darling, we talk about the price of fish in Jerusalem!' That was Ella's way of saying that we would just talk about whatever was on our minds at any moment.

My friendship with Ella was built on trust and respect. I remember that I would tell her my deepest fears and my most well-kept secrets, the things I didn't even disclose to my parents. I recall one day I came out to her as bisexual and she didn't have a clue what I was talking about. When I explained the concept to her she only replied with love, 'That's what people have told you that you are. You are simply Cael.' This one line meant so much, as I had feared she would be disappointed or upset that I was going against the religion. She didn't bat an eyelid; she accepted me for who I was. Ella would share stories of her upbringing, photos of her late husband and many wonderful moments and times of her life. She shared challenges and obstacles she overcame and would listen to my advances at school and eventually university.

Looking back, I can see the universe brought Ella and me together to gain from one another both wisdom and company. Growing up, I felt very alienated and lonely and she did too in her most senior years. Where I would lean on her for life skills, advice, nurturing and support, she would lean on me for practical help around the house and reminders about her purpose. This was all a process of give and take, learn and teach.

As I reflect on this profound relationship I'm reminded that Source never leaves us alone to figure life out. Source is very capable of bringing together bonds and people around us, and when you step back you will realise it's not a coincidence that you encounter the people you do in life. Source knows the right people to bring onto our path, and at the right time too. This is one way we can see Source at work through us: bringing other people into our life to better us, build us or shepherd us into new and exciting levels in our life. These relationships can have a great impact on us.

That's why relationships, tribe and community are extremely important and why we can find Source and Spirit right there among us when we have each other.

The importance of community and connection is emphasised across the span of all cultures and it's certainly what we need in the times we live in today. Showing up for people is one way we can strengthen our sense of community. It might simply be going to the dog park, joining a book club or volunteering for a charity. These relationships will link us into untapped wisdom that we may need in life out of the mouths of newfound friends.

If you aren't learning you are teaching, and if you aren't giving you are taking. This is the ebb and flow of life. There are seasons where you are in the seat of a student, learning many lessons, and in other seasons you will be called upon to teach and be the helper that gives to another person's cause or need.

Sadly, I lost touch with Ella as the years went by, but I believe the universe united us for those moments in our lives where we needed it most. Source can see directly into your life and know what things can be helped and can see into other people's lives and know how you can help them. Not a single opportunity is wasted by Source as it finds avenues and opportunities to position you in life for the journey of your assignment here on Earth.

Servant of the greater good

One winter morning several years ago, while I was conducting my daily rituals and prayers, I had a profound feeling that I wanted to be miraculously used to help people. I passionately verbalised to Source and the universe that I wanted to be used more to shift the world into love and make it a better place. I was so keen to be of service to assist humanity.

Later that same day, I was returning home from my studies. On my way I found a young woman lying on the steps of a dance studio. My heart sank because I thought she was dead. Next to her on the ground was her phone, its screen cracked.

'Excuse me, miss, are you okay?' I uttered as I approached her carefully.

'F*ck off and leave me alone.'

I could smell alcohol on her as I heard her speak to me.

I picked up her phone and could see that she had several missed calls from her mother. I dialled her mother and put the phone on speaker. I explained to her mother who I was and where I had found her daughter. Within minutes, the mother arrived. She was so relieved and thanked me for helping her daughter.

'She has an alcohol problem,' she told me.

This encounter showed me that sometimes what we do for others may seem invisible and small to us or to the world but it still makes an impact in someone's life. I knew anyone with a decent heart would have stopped to help that woman, but what if it had been someone with bad intentions? Source knew that I would be passing by that way and there's no way I'd leave a helpless and unconscious person by themselves. Although many other people had walked past her, they were busy on their phones. I had stopped without much thought.

That night I said to the universe, 'You really threw me in the deep end there, Spirit.'

I heard nothing back. However, I felt it wasn't the last time this would happen.

The next day, still a little shaken from my encounter with the woman, I decided to take a different route home. I jumped off the bus and turned the corner down the dirt alley to my house. In the distance I spotted a lady stumbling around, falling over and then getting back up. As I walked carefully closer, she collapsed into a heap on the rocky dirt and started crying. *What in the world?* I thought to myself. *What have I invoked into my life?!* I called the police and they immediately came to the woman's aid.

This was the second person I had helped off the street in two days! This was not what I had been imagining when I asked Source to show me more ways to help. I had envisioned working at a nice soup kitchen or something, but this was the furthest thing from that. It wasn't glamorous at all.

The reality is, this is how the universe can often work. If you position yourself to help, you may not always be able to see the good you've done or be rewarded for it immediately.

And, as with the examples above, sometimes you'll be called upon to help in unexpected ways, and you'll wonder, 'Why me?' but, as many can attest, the universe knows what it is doing. Eventually you will look back and realise that there was a lesson in the midst of that confusion, and that good things are coming your way. Some people observe this as karma. Do good and it will be returned to you. However, the opposite can occur as well.

Karma will handle it

When I was in high school in my small town, I was bullied incessantly for my dark skin and feminine attitude. One boy in particular was the ringleader. I attended Boy Scouts where this bully would give me a hard time. Week after week, I would go home crying, trying to pretend it never happened. One year we went on a Scout camp, where I was the literal black sheep in the division. I was never invited into the main tent with other boys to tell scary stories or bond over our favourite movies but was left alone in my tent. One day when we had to dig the hole for our outdoor toilet, this bully told me that he wished I could be buried with all the other 'sh*t' that would end up in the hole. This was the most hurtful thing I'd ever heard and I remember I didn't eat dinner that night and prayed the rest of the camp would be over quickly.

Throughout school, this bully would find ways to make

my life a living hell. He would go out of his way to catch the same bus as me in order to poke fun at me or walk on the path to move me off it as we walked as a Scout group in community events. I bottled up all of these interactions; I didn't want to tell anybody as I didn't think it was worth sharing. The last thing I remember this guy doing to me, along with another bully, was laughing as we all discussed what we wanted to do when we left school.

'Black people don't go to university,' he sneered.

Eleven years later, I had graduated from university and was working in psychology at a hospital. The ward I was working in was the suicide prevention unit, where I spoke to people with the highest risk and at the lowest point of their life.

One day I was called in to meet with the duty psychiatrist. He told me about a case that was about to present to Emergency and be assigned to me. I took the doctor's notes and returned to my desk to study the case. The patient had been raised in a drug- and alcohol-fuelled environment. He was battling drug abuse himself and was overcome by debt due to a gambling addiction.

A few hours after the presentation, I went over to the psychiatric ward to introduce myself to my new patient. It was commonplace to build rapport quickly and work closely with patients from the time they were admitted until they reached a point of stability in their mental health again. As I walked out of my office up the long hall to the ward, I realised I had forgotten to check the man's name to introduce myself.

I swiped my security tag, walked into the psychiatric ward and quickly ducked into the nurses' station to ask if the doctor was around and if he could remind me of the patient's name. The doctor was sitting right in front of me. He turned around, pointed to the dining room and said, 'You're here to see Harrison*.'

As I walked across the dining room, wearing my business attire and hospital ID, I could see the lanky man, sitting alone, glaring into a cup of tea. All of a sudden my heart sank as the name the doctor mentioned struck a familiar chord, as did his appearance. I thought, *Oh god, that's my Boy Scout bully.* As I approached the man, weirdly, a ray of sun coming in from the tall window behind him cast light directly down upon me.

'Harrison?' I said to him. 'I'm Cael, can I have a chat with you?'

He looked up from his cup with tired eyes, which quickly widened, like a deer caught in headlights. He glanced at me up and down. He had immediately recognised me.

'Cael? Why are you here?' he asked, quickly rubbing his hands through his hair as an obvious stress response.

'I'm here to help you,' I replied.

Harrison collapsed into tears, with his head resting on the edge of the table. I could feel the enormity of his realisation:

---

*   Not his real name.

the very man he had bullied all through high school was now standing before him, witnessing him at the lowest point in his life, as the professional help he needed.

Every weight I had felt while enduring the scorn of this man when we were kids vanished the moment I witnessed him discover I had risen from the ashes. There was no escaping the reality that Harrison was processing his years of ill treatment of me as I stood before him as his last chance to find help. Within moments of him collapsing into bitter tears, a nurse emerged and mouthed 'Thank you' to me, obviously dismissing me and suggesting it wasn't the right time.

As I walked back to my office, my body buzzed with concern for him, but also with a sense of pride in what I had achieved despite being bullied so intensely throughout my childhood and adolescence. It felt odd to be in a position of power before Harrison. The role reversal was nice but fleeting. At the end of the day, I was merely doing my job. It was obvious that Source had timed karma to teach the man something about the importance of treating everyone with care and respect.

Everything good or bad is tallied and noticed by Source, and, maybe not immediately but certainly in this life or the next, you will experience a karmic response to your actions. When Harrison was bullying me at school I could have started fights and punched him, or retaliated and made fun of his family or any other trivial thing, but I stayed radio silent and copped it on the chin.* And all of it was being stored up by Source and the universe to one day be a very important lesson for that man to learn. I don't think I'll ever hear how much that moment impacted him but it only took my observation of his face for me to read how utterly ashamed he felt about all those years ago. Sometimes Source will play the long game in timing lessons in our life and in the lives of others. It's not from a place of punishment or vindictiveness, but pure and unadulterated love.

I never saw Harrison again. He discharged himself shortly after the interaction he had with me and seemingly returned to his life.

Don't be afraid to take

One thing that I commonly see in people is their reluctance to ask for help. Countless times I have looked upon people in public struggling with the simplest things and have stepped in to help them. It's rare for people these days to ask for assistance out of fear of imposing on somebody else's 'busy' life. However, the magic is in finding the courage to ask. Source has an opportunity waiting for you behind your bravery. However, like the story above about Harrison, it's

---

* This was my way of handling it, but it's important to reiterate that help is available to anyone who is experiencing bullying or harassment. Please see the list of resources at the back of the book for more information.

often important to ask for help early on when you need it so you can prevent things from deteriorating to a very difficult place down the track.

We can't navigate this world alone; we need other people. As the saying goes, some people in your life are there for a reason, a season or a lifetime. You will often find the help of Source nestled in the onset of these new relationships. And you probably won't get something without paying for it in the way of a lesson or teaching. Source is too intelligent for that. It often wants to catch two birds with one stone. It wants to sharpen iron against iron and bring forth and unlock new character developments in us. Again, this is done through the currency of Source: giving and taking, learning and teaching.

Nothing is wasted

This life is all about learning and teaching, giving and taking. Even right now the universe is preparing to either use you to teach or show you something to learn. No relationship will be wasted, no opportunity will fall by the wayside. Interactions, whether big or small, can have incredible impacts on people's lives that can still be powerful years on. The more you open up to Source and the universe and render yourself not just a student of the world but also willing to share and teach what you have already learned, you will become a powerful force, and opportunities will seek you out.

This is all part of the human experience. Life, along with Spirit, is much more fulfilling and purposefully driven when you surrender to the phenomenon of learning and teaching, giving and taking. You're able to see the bigger picture and understand that even the smallest coincidences are purposefully aligned to impact two people's lives: you and the other person involved.

Once you can do this, Spirit will position you for blessings you would have never expected. When you're a willing participant in the life Source has created for you, and can offer help when you least expect it, you'll learn something you never thought you needed to know. These are moments that will come so subtly into your life that you'll feel the universe is tugging on your heart to be used for the greater good.

Three-minute exercise

Take a moment now to think of your loved ones and those around you. Write down things that they have taught you in your life simply by being a part of it. Then thank the universe for bringing these people into your life and, if you're willing, ask Spirit to use you more readily, not only in their lives to support them, but also in the lives of those who you don't know.

8

Decoding common signs, dreams and symbols

THE UNIVERSE IS CONSTANTLY trying to make contact with us and bring us new information through signs, dreams and symbols. However, if we aren't privy to its way of communicating we can often feel confused and overwhelmed by what a sign, symbol or dream might mean. The thing about signs and symbols is that they are markers in your life from Source to do two things: encourage you or get your attention. This is because Source does not meddle with your life without your permission. When you receive such visions, dreams, signs and symbols, either you are being given encouragement to continue on your way, or it's an invitation to allow Source to move in closer and take some of the load you're carrying off your back and support you with its own plan.

The following breakdown of dreams, signs and symbols is not an exhaustive list as there are thousands of them out there in the world and there is not enough room in this chapter to list them all! Here are some that I personally have recognised in my life as signs that the universe is using to communicate with me.

Dreams

Dreams are, beyond a doubt, communications from the spirit world. What better way to speak to you than when you are lying down and comatose? When you are asleep, you are able to block out the world around you and be presented with a theme, a story or narrative in a dream that you are likely to pay close attention to upon waking up. That is why Source will often use dreams to talk to us.

In saying this, though, sometimes dreams can just be a reflection of the subconscious mind. The number-one thing I get asked about dreams is how to know whether the contents of a dream comes from the subconscious (that is, you processing your own current time in life) or are a spiritual sign. I answer this by saying that it is all about how you awake from the dream. If you wake from a dream panicked and worried or feeling upset, often that dream will not be stemming from the spiritual world but be a subconscious psychological process that you are dealing with. These dreams from the subconscious can be interpreted, too, but not through the lens of signs from Source. However, if you wake up deeply rested, curious about your dream, and with a sense of purpose or as if you've been given a 'message', then it's likely that you made contact with the spiritual world in your sleep.

Back to school

Have you ever dreamed you were back in the schoolyard of your primary school or high school? Or maybe you were on the school bus, inside a classroom or talking to a teacher. Dreaming about being back at school is a sign that you are in a learning chapter of your life and that Source is encouraging you to take what you have learned in the past and activate or use it in the present. The back-to-school dream can often happen to those who might be wondering why so many things seem to be happening all at once, with challenge after challenge presenting itself. This is because teaching methods at many schools involve new concepts being repeated until you can grasp them. The same is true for the spiritual realm. You will be shown a school dream if you are not grasping something that Source is trying to tell you.

The mother

If you have dreams about a mother figure or a maternal presence, this is often a sign from the universe that the divine feminine energy of Mother Nature is stepping closer to you. It's a time to let your life flow rather than keeping things rigid and planned. The mother figure is trying to tell you that even if you are not sure where things are taking you in the current moment in your life, it's important to accept and surrender to the flow of life. The divine feminine is calling you to slow down, take stock of your current life situation, and consider where your broader life plan is going. After dreaming about mothers, you might find that you want to take a step back from your social engagements and retreat inwards for a while – for example, you might skip a weekend brunch with friends in order to practise yoga or spend time journalling. By surrendering to the 'flow of life' you will see the world around you afresh. You will start to see what fits and what doesn't, what is worth working towards, and what is worth leaving behind. (See also 'A pattern of 1s' on page 107.)

The father

Dreams about a father figure or a paternal presence are a sign from the universe that your path and life, whether you see it or not, is taking shape. You are in the midst of setting up strong foundations. For example, if you began a new path of education or training, the father might appear in your dreams as a sign to say that you have what it takes and to encourage you to remain diligent and focused. If you're at a crossroads in life, the father figure can also provide wisdom and guidance about the next stage of your journey. After you wake from such a dream you might feel as though you have your answer inside your heart about which path to take.

The friend

If you dream about a friend, regardless of the content (or the friend!), it's about your relationship with your spirit guide. Spirit guides appear as friends because they see themselves as your equal, wanting to guide and show you how to navigate things that are practical. You might see friends in your dreams while you are unemployed and applying for jobs or before you give birth or get married or achieve another milestone. In times of change and upheaval, this is Spirit's way of reassuring and supporting you.

The ocean

Dreaming of the ocean is a positive sign from Spirit for many reasons. One of the most common reasons you might dream of the ocean is because it is a sign of untapped potential – it means that Spirit is encouraging you to explore and unlock possibilities and opportunities that you may not have considered before. No matter our age, visiting the seaside can be exciting because of the fun, playful activities we can engage in at the beach. Dreaming of going to the ocean or swimming in the ocean means that Spirit is encouraging you to be more curious about your life and the world around you. If your dream involves drowning or encountering a dangerous animal, this could simply be the universe's way of acknowledging any apprehension you might be having about new possibilities, and helping you to see a way forward.

The forest

To dream about the forest signifies a special time of personal development and introspection. Spirit is asking you to examine your current thoughts, feelings and motivations. You might dream of visiting a forest or being lost or even chased through one when you feel stuck about your current situation. Perhaps you are in a relationship with several hurdles to overcome, a family dilemma you need support about, or you're bored of your longstanding career. Dreams of this nature mean that Spirit is encouraging you to slow down and inspect your current needs. Spirit is also reminding you that it's okay to reconsider the path you're on. Sometimes it's okay to take a step backwards.

The tall peak

A dream of a mountain (or anything of great height, such as a skyscraper or staircase) is a divine sign that is most sacred. It represents one primary challenge you might be facing, and dreaming about one challenge means that Source is taking responsibility for it. Source is telling you that you're facing this challenge not to punish or distress you but to give you an opportunity for personal growth. You're not only growing through this challenge but you are also being stepped up to a new frequency in order to accomplish greater things. For example, you might see a mountain in your dreams if you are struggling to sell your house or your grades at school or university are declining. Source is saying to you, 'We see you are struggling, and we are going to help you grow. When you wake up, invoke us to help!'

The celebrity

If you have dreamed about a celebrity, consider the craft or art this person produces. For example, if you keep having dreams about a singer, think about the songs that they sing. Perhaps there's one in particular that has recently been playing on repeat in your head. What is the song about? What does it mean to you? Similarly, if it was an actor, have you recently watched one of their films? What were its themes? Which character did that actor play? Did you identify with that character? It could be tempting to ignore such a dream, but with a little bit of digging and introspection you could find that the dream, and why it was shown at this time in your life, makes a lot of sense to you.

Pregnancy

Dreaming about pregnancy is a clear sign from Spirit that you are cooking up something new in the near future. Perhaps a new relationship is on the horizon, or a promotion that you've been working towards, a degree you're about to receive, or an idea is about to take flight as a side gig or business partnership. Or even – surprise, surprise – a baby!

Falling

Dreaming of falling into nothingness and startling awake in a cold sweat is normal. In fact, it's a sign that Spirit has recognised you are taking on too much in your life. Are you feeling overwhelmed or spread too thinly? It's time to pull back and take a break. Spirit is trying to remind you that you are only one person and many of the responsibilities that you take on are often beyond what is necessary. This type of dream is also a sign that you might be feeling unsupported at this time. Reach out to those you love and see how they will naturally support you.

Teeth falling out

This dream occurs when Spirit has seen that you are holding pent-up anxiety. This anxiety is usually in the form of your sense of productivity or purpose being called into question. Smiling is a way of showing pride and confidence, and when anything hinders our sense of a good smile, it could mean that something is hindering our pride. Spirit is acknowledging this and reminding you of your potency, competency, and the strength and power that you hold.

Being chased

Being chased is a sign that Spirit can see that demands are creeping up on you. Perhaps you have a looming debt that is worrying you or a job interview coming up that you feel unprepared for. This dream is an acknowledgement that these things will soon pass – but you do need to address them. Ignoring something will not make it go away. It might feel disconcerting and unsafe to be chased but it's really a way for you to recognise and see that once you have made the effort and done the work required, these things can be corrected and resolved.

Snakes or dangerous animals

These dreams can indicate mental health challenges. It could be common to have these dreams when you are battling a wave of depression or feeling more anxious than usual. You might dream that these animals are trying to harm you but Spirit is using this dream to remind you that you are not in danger when you treat these animals right. You have control over your mind and can ensure that you are mentally safe by engaging in regular and intentional self-care practices, and seeking support from a professional when you need it.

Recurring plotlines

Are you having the same dream over and over again from night to night? Perhaps you're repeatedly being chased by snakes or your teeth keep falling out. A recurring plotline is Spirit trying to draw your attention to the meaning behind the dreams that they are sending. It's like a neon sign right in front of you, asking you to pay close attention.

How to decode dreams with Spirit

Perhaps you're sure that your dream was a message from Spirit, but you want to delve deeper into what it means and why Spirit sent it to you. What better way to do this than to ask the sender! There are several ways you can do this.

You could simply ask Spirit to communicate the meaning of your dream in your mind throughout the day. You could also draw upon a deck of oracle cards. Oracle cards are similar to tarot cards and can offer more detailed insight into Spirit's message. Be sure to follow the instructions that come with your cards, as they can vary from deck to deck.

Another method of decoding your dreams is using a pendulum. A pendulum is any weighted matter hung from a fixed point in order to let it swing back and forth. If you want to know if a message was from Spirit, you might use the pendulum to ask a series of yes-or-no questions aloud. The pendulum will answer by swinging side to side (no) or forwards and backwards (yes).

Signs and symbols

If Spirit can't reach you when you're asleep, then there's every chance it will try to contact you when you're awake, through signs and symbols that are hiding in plain sight. However, you'd be surprised just how many people are so oblivious to these signs that they go about their normal lives unaware that the universe is in a full dialogue with them. That being said, it's important to know that Spirit isn't just going to pop out from behind the curtain of invisibility and start speaking to you. Spirit will most likely communicate with you indirectly, through a series of symbols and signs. The following is certainly not an exhaustive list of these signs and symbols, but a collection of what I have found to be the most common.

Spirit numbers

Spirit numbers, or synchronised numbers, are a phenomenon of repeated numbers appearing to you in the world. For example, you glance at your microwave clock one evening to see it display 11:11. Or the following morning you find yourself catching the 10:10 train into the city. Seeing these patterns emerge from numbers can be so surprising and at times overwhelming because it's a repetition that can feel so significant. Here are the most important ones to know.

A pattern of 1s

This is a symbol of divine intervention; a clear sign that it isn't only on the physical plane that you are being supported but also in the spiritual world. This number serves to remind you that you have the help of divine guides that are pulling strings from behind the scenes to shift things for you.

A pattern of 2s

This is the number of the divine feminine. Seeing repeating 2s is your reminder from Spirit that mothering and nurturing energies are present and willing to step in and assist you. You might be feeling that your life is swirling around with uncertainty; however, a reminder of this number can function as a check-in from Spirit to say that if a mother or grandmother is in spirit, they are close by or have heard your prayer or request to them.

A pattern of 3s

This number represents past, present and future. It is associated with good luck, and means that Spirit is endowing you with favourable energy. There is a unity within this number as well – think of the mind, body and soul. This is Spirit letting you know that you have the approval and favour of your spirit team, guides or Source that the direction in which you are taking things is being supported.

A pattern of 4s

This is a masculine sign from Spirit. It invokes the four elements of earth, air, fire and water and the cardinal points of north, south, east and west. This number is Spirit reassuring you, that logistically, you are going to be provided for and what might not seem apparent right now is about to be revealed. It can also be interpreted as an encouragement to use your intellect and inner strength to navigate the major areas of your life.

A pattern of 5s

This is a sacred symbol from Spirit reminding you of your health, vitality and light. Even if you don't feel these things right now, the number 5 is a reminder that you can access and invoke them through manifestation and intention. It's like a hug from the universe acknowledging where you are and what you have sacrificed to get there.

A pattern of 6s

It's easy to fear a repetition of the number 6 due to the work of Hollywood or a religious upbringing that associated '666' with evil. But don't be alarmed. This number is associated with your ego. Perhaps it's calling you to reflect on how you are handling things and if you are truly aligned with your values and morals at this time. For example, have you been blaming your partner for something when you're actually the one at fault? It's time for accountability. Usually, 666 appears to those who are deeper in their practice of shadow work and inner healing, who can take constructive criticism from Spirit.

A pattern of 7s

This symbol represents determination. If you see this sign it is a reminder that you sit in the seat of power in your life and that deep down you know where you are going and why you are here. You are the creator and arbiter of your next steps and Source is reminding you through these numbers that you will be able to rely on your own intelligence or inner compass to make any decisions that lie ahead of you.

A pattern of 8s

This symbol is a reminder to rest and renew. You don't have to be 'on' all the time. It's common for people to feel that they are always a mother or always a boss but it doesn't matter how demanding these roles might be, it's important to carve out time for yourself to rejuvenate and bask in a space of rest.

A pattern of 9s

This is the symbol for commitment and completion, and is a reminder from Source to finish what you started. Whether it's building a business, a family or a house, this number is an entreaty to stay the course, and to do it with all your heart. It might take stepping away from distractions and some willpower but you will thank yourself when you have finished that which you started.

A pattern of 10s

This is a symbol of fortune and abundance. It means that a wave of abundance is coming. If you see this number it is a reminder that your manifestations or whatever you are creating will be highly profitable. It may not be in the form of directly receiving money but in the ability to produce and create wealth. This could be from business opportunities, a promotion or creative endeavours.

A pattern of 11s

A recurring number 11 (particularly 11:11) is a powerful number sequence and is often associated with big changes that are dawning in your life. For example, several major life changes might be about to happen all at once – a new home or relocation, career growth or promotion, new love or a milestone in your relationship or for your family. It will often appear at the cusp of a new decade.

The feather

A feather is a divine symbol sent collectively from your spirit team, which comprises your loved one in spirit, Source and Spirit. If you find a feather, this is a reminder that they recently heard you ask them for guidance, or that you are being supported at this time by them. It could be a reminder that, even if you feel lost and alone, they are there on the sidelines to support you.

Déjà vu

Having déjà vu is often a sign from Source and your loved ones in spirit. Because they exist in the spirit realm and cannot command your complete and undivided attention, they will often move closer and drop new downloads of encouragement. When a spirit has done this, it often feels like the phenomenon of déjà vu.

Finding money

Finding money can be a sign from Source to you. Not only is it immediately a new item of abundance, it is also a sign that there is more on the way. Finding $20 or a small amount in the street while nobody is around is a sign that your frequency is aligned to receive a new form of financial increase if you are willing and ready to make the effort and put in the time required.

Party decorations

Let's say you're walking down the street and you see a party decoration, such as a balloon, flying off by itself. This is a sign from Spirit that it is celebrating and cheering you on, commending you on your amazing recent achievements or actions. If you see streamers or party poppers in a street when there is no party around, it is simply an acknowledgement from Spirit that you are being admired from beyond.

Someone has or wears the same thing as you

If you notice that somebody is wearing the same shirt as you or has the same iPhone case or shoes, this is actually Spirit reminding you of your unique qualities. It's always a moment of wonder when we see someone else with something that we ourselves own. We often think we are the only ones who own such a thing. When this occurs, it's a reminder that you are impacting the world and your family and friends in your own way in this season and it's something to be commended for. The person you are helping would not be the same without your care and support.

A stopped clock or watch

If your clock stops at a particular time, it is often a sign from Spirit. If your watch stops at eight o'clock, it is no coincidence. Look up the meaning of the number that your clock stopped on and see how its meaning can be applicable to your life right now.

Ringing in the ear

Another sign from Spirit can be the sensation of ringing in the ear. If this occurs, the ringing should be neither unpleasant nor intrusive, as is the way of Spirit. This might occur when you are in moments of high thought, contemplating spiritual questions; or it may occur when you are feeling a strong, high-vibration emotion such as happiness, compassion and love. Any ringing in the ear should stir curiosity, not concern. If it occurs frequently, you might need to see a doctor.

Keep your eyes open

From the perspective of Spirit, you are never alone. It is constantly finding ways to reach out to you. There are hundreds more signs out there in the world and you might become privy to them as you step closer to Spirit.

Three-minute exercise

Take three minutes to ask Spirit if there are any signs not mentioned in this chapter that might be evident in your life. If you do this while closing your eyes, you might notice imagery or a story playing in your mind. Look at the things that manifest within the vision from Spirit and realise they are being employed to both encourage you and grab your attention for a specific reason. Remember to not be alarmed but allow them to show you what these signs are for. If you can meet them with an open and curious heart, they will willingly assist!

9

Manifesting

MANY PEOPLE ARE CONTENT to move through life happily accepting whatever comes their way, whether that be a partner, a promotion or a pet. The thing is, by this point, you've probably recognised that you're not the average person, because you can sense that there is something beyond what is here in the physical realm. Perhaps you feel your life is yet to achieve particular milestones or goals that inspire you and others. This is where manifesting can help.

What is manifesting?

Manifesting is the ability to call forth into existence what is waiting for you! It is a superpower that can bring anything that you desire into your life – if done properly. Manifestation is also known as the Law of Attraction. The Law of Attraction states that your thoughts, feelings and beliefs can attract into your life positive or negative realities. For example, when I was sixteen years old I realised that I wanted to work in a hospital, specialising in mental health. As I went out and studied in order to obtain the qualifications that would align myself to that reality, I also visualised what it would be like to work at a hospital – how much I would be paid, the experiences I would have, etc. I even visualised the lunch room and the conversations I would have with my colleagues over a sandwich! Lo and behold, nine years later there I was sitting in the lunch room working the job I always wanted. This was because I maintained a positive mindset and always believed that there was an opportunity ahead of me, waiting for me to step into it. The thing about successful people is they work hard to remain consistently positive and optimistic about their life and their future. This in itself creates a frequency ready to receive.

'Why does all of this work?' you might wonder. Well, the simple fact is that Source deeply desires for you to have better and to get better. Many people might think mani-festing is selfish and all about feeding our egos, but that is a very narrow way of considering the bigger reason mani-festing works.

How to manifest

The most important part of manifesting is to maintain the idea that you already have the thing you desire. You already have the job, the house, the family, the partner, the career, etc. that you are trying to manifest. Once you have conceptualised your desire, you should begin to act like it's yours. Make it part of your everyday life. If you behave as if you already have what you want, then what you want will seek you out. There isn't a set time of day you need to sit down and manifest – you should be manifesting all the time. Below is a guide to help you be more specific with what you want.

Career

When you are manifesting success or progression in your career, it's important to understand that anything to do with your career is always going to involve other people. Whether it is cutting their hair, bagging their groceries, representing them legally or selling them a house, you will be involved in the business of helping people. When you manifest for your career with visualisation, it's important to visualise how people will feel working with you. Imagine working alongside incredible colleagues who find your work ethic inspiring, your ideas valuable and your presence magnetic. If you're looking to excel in a corporate career, imagine the kinds of events you will be invited to and spend a moment visualising the networking opportunities or meet-ups. Feel the excitement when you log in to your bank account and see that your dream company is paying your salary. Walk yourself through an entire day of work in your desired career. What you would wear, how you would do your nails and hair, and what way you arrive to work. Will you drive a fancy Mercedes into your reserved parking spot or will you ride your bike? Or will you have the flexibility to work from home? Visualise and feel deeply what experiences you would have that would make you feel satisfied in this career. Consider what conversations you'll have coming home to your partner at dinner about the work you do, imagine your kids telling other parents and teachers that their mother or father is X, Y or Z.

Do you see how specific I am being? It is crucial for you to be as specific as possible so that you can get exactly what you want. The universe is waiting for your order and if you're not specific enough you might not receive exactly what you want.

Before I interviewed for my hospital job I dressed professionally on the weekends or whenever I was in public and imagined that I already had the job I wanted. I would drive my car to the carpark of the hospitals at which I wanted to work and practise getting out of the car as if I were starting my shift. (I can't imagine how many security guards would have watched on in total confusion at my antics but I'm sure they've endured far worse!)

In hindsight, I probably looked and acted like a person in need of some thoughts and prayers in those moments. However, these manifestation activities that I did, consistently and intentionally, landed me my dream job. I imagined confidently walking into the job interview and wowing the panel with my answers and being called back right away. And, the fact is, all of this happened. I remember a comment my new employer made to me over the phone when they offered me the job: 'You were the only candidate that dressed professionally and made a strong impression.' This comment made me feel chuffed and I realised that the power of manifesting what I wanted them to perceive me as had worked!

Romantic relationships

You can manifest romantic relationships very easily. When it comes to romance, along with visualising, it can also help to write down a description of your love. Start with how you want them to look, and traits that truly get you interested in a person. Write down what you hope you will have the strongest bond over. Perhaps you want someone who lives an exciting life of constant travel, or someone who loves philosophy and thought, or someone who wants to have a family relatively soon. List all the things you want in a relationship and don't feel guilty about being specific.

Once you have your list, visualise this person in your mind's eye. Imagine how it feels to be held emotionally in the relationship; how it feels to be loved by this person. Feel their supportive words in the form of text messages or chats after a long day. Visualise someone wholeheartedly committed to your best interests – for example, someone who can support you and be by your side as you heal from trauma. Consider the milestones and achievements you both will celebrate: birthdays, anniversaries, life goals and more.

Let your heart go wild in fully and completely designing this lover on paper and in your mind. Allow yourself to antici-pate encountering them soon and know that upon meeting them you will instantly feel a connection. This is your lover, your life partner and your closest friend.

When manifesting and visualising your romantic rela-tionship it's also important that you make yourself findable. Some people spend their life manifesting love, but it's not enough to stay put and hope someone will fall into your lap. If you never venture beyond your comfort zone, you're unlikely to end up on your lover's radar.

There are lots of ways to put yourself out there – both online, through dating apps and websites, or the old-fashioned way, by getting out of the house. Head to where you would love to meet someone. Are you an avid gardener? Stop by a potting demonstration at your local plant nursery on the weekend and see who shows up. And shaking up old habits and places might mean that you bump into someone unexpected, too. You could try getting your morning coffee from a new café, or, if you like fitness, jump out of the yoga room for a while and pretend that you actually want to do some weights in the weights room.

You have to be where people are to find love. If you can manifest and visualise your future relationship wholeheartedly, don't waste that magic by staying undiscoverable – go out in the world and allow that energy and power to send you into the embrace of someone completely amazing for you.

And don't forget to let Source guide you. Ask Spirit how you might be more successful in finding love. Does it believe you'll be more successful online or offline? In your hometown or further afield? Will your love be someone completely new or someone from your past?

Becoming a parent

If you're looking to expand your family, here are some of the words of advice I've given to clients who have been hoping to bring the joy of a new baby into the world. Visualise not only finding out the news that you (or your partner) are pregnant or have been 'OK'd for adoption' but actually arriving home with your baby. This is a powerful act of faith.

Along with this, purchase a onesie in a baby's size. As you manifest and actionably work towards bringing a child into your world, regularly put the onesie in the laundry, as if the baby already lives in your house and is part of the laundry routine. Begin speaking to the child in the universe as if it already exists. This will make you look completely silly in front of your partner or anyone else around you, but don't worry about that. Play music for babies or kids' TV shows for a good 30 minutes a week.

Every time you carry out one of these activities, make sure you take the time to visualise the child being present in your life. As you visualise and manifest radically like this, you are sending signals and a frequency to the universe that you would like to be a parent. And there is another element to manifesting, which I will come to in the next section.

Money

If you want to manifest wealth, it's important to start with a blank page in your mindset. As of right now, I want you to consider that you don't just have a couple of physical banks here on Earth. Would you accept it, today, if I told you that your future money or riches are stored above you in a bank? An invisible bank that nobody has access to but you. When you require money from it, simply visualise the vault door opening and you walking inside and taking what you need.

Another way that I like to visualise wealth is by considering how the money will be used and why it's important to you. $20,000 is not much use if it's never going to be spent. Complete the loop of manifesting and imagine what you will buy with the money. Consider not only how this money will make you feel but also how others will feel around you. Avoid thinking that money will make others jealous of you, but instead focus on how your money might inspire other people or perhaps how it could be used to help people altruistically.

As hard as it might seem to step away from fixed mindsets about money, it's important to try to do so. This is particularly true when it comes to narratives about money that we were raised to believe. For example, 'money doesn't grow on trees' might be something you were told as a child, but at its heart it's a money block that can limit your ability to imagine your own wealth. Keep an open mind, visualise what you want, and see what happens.

The key to manifesting

The special sauce when it comes to manifesting is that you need to sell your concept to the universe. Asking for a baby, money or help with your career is fine; however, you need to make a case to Source for why this is important. You have to convince the universe that whatever you want is in line with what the universe is willing to help with. For example, asking for $20,000 because you simply want it will be a sure-fire way to hear and see a big fat 'no' from the universe. So instead, tell the universe how you intend to improve the world through your acquisition of wealth. Tell the universe you want a child not just because you want one but because this child will grow up and make the world a better place.

If you're seeking advancement in your career, tell the universe that you're willing to work hard to help people, you will use your career to inspire or assist others, and you will always be grateful for the opportunities that the universe is sending your way. By positioning your desires in this way, you will also gain a clearer understanding of the higher purpose attached to them.

The money, baby or career has an ultimate purpose and you simply want to align with that purpose and assert that you are the arbiter, the only key person that this can be channelled through.

An essential superpower

Ultimately, I believe any spiritual person needs to manifest. The importance of manifesting cannot be overstated, and is a superpower we must all practise so that our divine needs, plans and destinies are activated and brought into the world. Manifesting takes our lives by the reins and steers us towards our greater potential.

You might be wondering, 'Cael, how does me manifesting my lover make the universe excited?' Well, when you have a companion you can be supported tenfold in your purpose or potential. Having a baby can catapult you into a new sense of responsibility that will burn away old traits that no longer serve you and bring out amazing traits that will inspire your family and others. A better career or more wealth is yet another crucial thing the universe wants for you because some of the most successful people in the world are able to make a positive impact through charitable work and philanthropy.

However, the key is that we must be willing to manifest what we want and to believe that there is actually a plan within our desire. If you zoom out and see that your manifesting efforts and attempts are more valuable to Source on a macro level, you will position your visualisation and the way you ask for these things in a whole new way. You will start to feel incredible purpose spring forth from the universe to you because even your most abstract and luxurious desires have consequences that could better help, advance or evolve the world in ways you're yet to see.

Three-minute exercise

Spend three minutes with Spirit writing down your deepest or even your most luxurious desires to manifest. Once you've done this, connect how each item on your list will impact something or someone positively if it is brought into your life through your manifesting.

PART THREE

Looking beyond

10

Where did they go?

As WE MOVE INTO the third and final part of the book, it's time to lift our minds and step beyond the physical world that surrounds us to further contemplate the spirit world beyond.

I've touched upon the existence of realms surrounding the planet we are all walking around on, and many of us might not have given much serious thought to what happens after death until someone close to us dies and we are forced to confront the possibilities. We might feel anxious about what has happened to them, and can't fathom that they could have just disappeared. Or perhaps you have experienced your own brush with death, such as a serious illness or accident, which has made you take stock of what's around you and reflect on what could be awaiting one day on the other side.

Having been privileged to speak to thousands of clients around the world in my work, one of the most common questions I'm asked is where a loved one has gone after they've departed their physical body.

A common question that's impossible to answer

A paradise full of alacritous virgin brides? An island that flows with an abundance of milk and honey? (For the vegans this might sound a bit hellish!) Or a glorious cloud of harp-playing angels and harmonic choirs? Where *do* we go when we 'bite the dust', 'give up the ghost' or 'kick the bucket'?

The simple answer to that is a confident and factual, 'Nobody has a clue.' Not a single person has returned to tell the tale, have they? Even near-death experiences simply align with the cultures of the people who experience them. Isn't it strange that Hindus who 'die' report seeing Lord Krishna, while Christians see Jesus Christ, Muslims see Allah and atheists see, well, nothing?

Not even I, as a seasoned psychic medium, can confidently know what our loved ones are experiencing when they pass. I know that they can see and hear us and even communicate with us, but as for the full extent of what it's like *over there*, your guess is as good as mine.

So, as for where we go and what happens to our inner

being when we pass away, these questions have been around for tens of thousands of years and any attempt to answer them will lead you down a rabbit hole of millions of options. As long as human beings walk this Earth we will continually be trying to make sense of what we don't know. It is in our nature; we are thinking beings. We are capable of thinking for ourselves and believing in what makes the most logical or emotional sense to us.

Given that nobody really knows what happens after we pass, it means that all beliefs are equally valid. So, if it is the idea of heaven that brings you joy and meets your need for closure, then that's what you should believe in. Perhaps reincarnation as a response to karma fits well within your soul – if so, go ahead and believe it! You've got every right. Conversely, if a belief is blocking your joy, if it is arresting any prospect of you finding hope or closure, you have the freedom to walk away from it. You have the opportunity to replace it with what truly feels right for you.

They live on

Here, I'm sharing the closest thing to what I believe happens when we die, and what I perceive is occurring when I communicate with the departed.

But before that, I want to share a story about something that happened during a client reading that provides an insightful look into the spirit world. The client was looking to connect with the spirit of her father, who had suffered from Alzheimer's disease and had been a widower for eight years before his death. His passing was the kind we all hope to have – he was with family, and, in a wistful moment, his last breath was taken and he fell into his fate.

He had been a solitary man, with little left but his daughter, who was right alongside him in the hospital. She was a professional singer, and in the quiet hospital room the sound of her singing could be heard. It wasn't just any nice song – in fact, it was a song that she had written for her father. It was common for him to ask her to sing this song over and over when the thought of his imminent passing gripped his reality and he needed reassurance.

In the reading I told the woman what her father kept saying in the spirit world: 'Mum finished the song.' Initially, I had no idea what the meaning of this assuring message was, but my client understood it immediately. She explained to me that the last time she ever sang it to her father, she realised that he had passed away before she made it to the second verse.

Spirit described to me that, at the moment of passing, the sound of the man's daughter's voice slowly faded. At the same time, his wife's voice, singing the same song, slowly faded in. The remainder of the song that had been enjoyed on Earth was finished by his wife in the spirit world. The man described entering the spirit world at the speed of an eye-blink; that the moment your eyelids meet is the instant that you find yourself aware that you are in the afterlife with your loved ones. He told me that it is not startling at the beginning – it's as if you are left on your own for a brief moment until you realise what's going on, and then one by one, your loved ones will approach you and greet you, exactly as you remember them from the physical world.

Aboriginal and Torres Strait Islander peoples have their own beliefs about death, and consider this experience to be merely a transition into another life – an afterlife that is very similar to their lives before death. This belief of my forefathers seems the simplest and most accurate way that I can describe what it looks and sounds like, based on my connections as a psychic medium. From what I can gather from spirits I have communicated with, when you pass away, nothing major really occurs – there is no glowing angel with wings appearing to take you to heaven, no male god waiting to speak to you with a booming voice. Instead, what seems to occur is a reunion with your loved ones and the souls you remember. When you pass, you won't be alone in that moment but are met by your spirit guide that is always around or beside you first. This is usually an ancestor or loved one.

You will have no more need of the physical body. You will live on as a spirit among your people but also integrate lovingly with others. You will help your earthly children and your future descendants to live their lives by playing a powerful role in some way as a guardian over them. Practically, you will elevate towards a position of a guide or ancestral helper.

There is the option to reincarnate, but, in my experience, that is rare, and for those who deeply want to be able to make big and impactful changes on Earth. Perhaps that is why you're here on Earth: you were one of the spirits that decided to come back, to have another go at changing something for the better here.

It's also worth mentioning that I've had only a handful of readings where I've not had a spirit step forward or be able to be contacted. When it has occasionally happened, the client will usually tell me that this has happened before with many other mediums, and they were told that their loved one had reincarnated as their granddaughter or someone else – hence why they could not access them in the spirit realm. (More on reincarnation a little further down.)

What is consistent throughout the readings I do is that a spirit will often share that they have been constantly moving around back and forth from various loved ones in the physical realm, depending on where they are most needed. This could be across borders into other countries to visit people who they love, or just within one household.

As mentioned in Chapter 2, it's important to remember that a constant self of ours exists that is the higher self, or what I like to label the non-human aspect of us. It's us without the psychological chemicals, the childhood attachment styles and many other things that form the foundation of what we identify as 'ourselves'. The view that is shared among Native Americans and Australian First Nations peoples supports the view that it is almost like when we incarnate to Earth, we have two spirits; when we depart we return to the 'Great Spirit', like most rivers returning to the greater source of water which is the ocean.

Reincarnation

Imagine a colour that can't be found on a rainbow. Imagine a shade that doesn't exist. You can't, right? The logical conclusion would therefore be, well, there are no other colours than the colours we know.

Now imagine being dead. Although not the same, the mere thought of not existing doesn't make any sense, in the same way that we don't know what other colours there are. The closest you'd get is being unconscious, but even then, it's possible to have small recollections of things said or done during the time you were out. The same goes for sleeping, but even then, our internal 'clock' keeps ticking, just at a different rate than normal, which is why we can train our brain to wake us up without an alarm. Just as we find it unimaginable to think of 'new' colours, we can say the same about death. The human consciousness cannot comprehend not existing, ergo we feel it must exist in one way or another.

So, because we can't imagine not existing or existing in an afterlife we aren't sure of, we fall back on the idea of reincarnation – that we live again and again – because living is all we have ever known. Many people these days are inclined to believe in reincarnation, drawn to the idea that their loved one is 'recycled' as a soul and returns to Earth reincarnated as another member of the family, an animal or another sentient being. This is a common teaching in the Eastern religions.

Many Indigenous people view life as a self-sustaining cycle, a little like the water cycle on Earth. Water flows through the stages of evaporation, rising into the atmosphere, forming clouds and then raining down again. You may not reincarnate as *you* with all of your features again in a new life immediately, but you might be importantly used in another way up in the atmosphere. Imagine all the little water droplets and molecules rising to the atmosphere as if they were souls: some are moved around to achieve many different things and travel to many different places but they are all but a part of one big entity: H_2O. Even the body will return to the soil and become part of the Earth again.

Reincarnation is one of the afterlives that makes sense to me, as it reiterates the fact that no higher being or force is responsible for you but *you*. This echoes the teachings of Chapter 5, as well: you are the person who is navigating, creating and living in your own karma and dharma. It makes sense that if you were to pass away and then be reincarnated, you would live a happy life as a reward for your good acts in the one preceding it, or face a litany of misfortunes if you weren't good in the last one.

Nothing to fear

'Oh, I've done it many times,' said my friend. We were talking about death and confabbing on what we believed was 'over there' when we crossed. This friend of mine is very self-aware and has a deep knowledge and curiosity about the spirit world. 'It's as natural as getting up out of a chair,' he continued. He was referring to what happened the moment we die.

I was amazed at his resolute, confident answer. It was as if he were explaining to me the voracity of a waterpark slide that I am trying to muster up the courage to attempt while he had been down it many times before. His confidence on the topic often serves as an anchor for my own uncertainty. He strongly believes in past lives and claims to vividly remember how he had died in each of his lifetimes. He asserts that fear is the last thing that we need to have when it comes to thinking about passing, and in fact, there are not a lot of things I can count that he is afraid of.

If you think about it, when we get up out of a chair, we don't ask, 'Will my knees carry me?' or 'Is the ground stable?', we simply stand up and carry on with where we were going.

My friend believes that's what death feels like: you simply stand up out of your body in some respects and keep going on your journey in the spirit realm until you are ready or willing to incarnate again. The universe, from my friend's perspective, treats us like a fully grown adult. Some people believe we should be punished or judged for the mistakes we make in life. That view, in his eyes, is juvenile and makes us weak. We need to stand tall in the universe and, as a single piece of that universe, look it square in the eye. We need to realise judging or criticising doesn't exist in the spirit world because it is a pointless exercise. We are in the driver's seat and we will grow and learn profoundly, as we have done before.

If you've lost someone dear to you and are wondering how to continue loving and honouring them now they're no longer physically here, that's what we'll look at in the next chapter.

Three-minute exercise

Who's waiting for you? Spend a brief moment reflecting on who would be the first person who approaches you in spirit. Write down one thing in sentence form in a journal that you believe they might say to you first when you reunite with them again.

11

Honouring Spirit

WHEN THE SUMMER RAINS and typhoons are in full swing in China, one evening each August is set aside as a time of solemn remembrance for those who have passed. Lanterns are placed on water so that lost spirits may find their way by following the floating lights. This is known as the Ghost Festival.

In Ecuador, stick figures made of bread are placed beside the graves to honour the spirits who have passed on.

Here in Australia, within Aboriginal and Torres Strait Islander cultures, saying the full name of a person who has recently departed is avoided, and showing an image of a person who has passed is considered disrespectful. First Nations peoples will often practise what is called Sorry Time or Sorry Business, a period of solemn mourning that lasts for days as loved ones gather from far and wide to support the family who has lost one of its members.

Across the world, you will find a variety of ways that we as humans deal with and pay respect to a person's death, as well as honour the memory of their life. These practices are special and unique to all the people and cultures they belong to, but what they share is the ability to bind us together in the human experience as we acknowledge death.

Honouring with our words

One of the most common questions about departed loved ones I receive at the end of my psychic medium readings is, 'What do they want me to do with their estate?' It doesn't matter what country I am giving readings in or what culture whoever I'm meeting with is part of, a departed loved one's belongings seem to be the first thing most people want to get right. During some readings I'll find that loved ones are quite explicit about what they want, whereas in others I get a curt 'Whatever you like – I have no need for it now.'

However, a person's possessions are not what matters when it comes to truly honouring their spirit. It's not the opulent demonstrations of wealth through mausoleums or gold-trimmed headstones that really show we care. Instead, honouring Spirit is all in how we choose to remember them and how we speak of them as they live on in the spirit realm.

When I worked at the hospital, I undertook suicide prevention training. Part of the training involved being educated about ways to talk about suicide. A professor in her mid-thirties from out of town came to speak to us, equipped with the usual assortment of pamphlets and a slightly dated PowerPoint presentation.

'How many of you have known people who have committed the crime of suicide?' she asked.

Hands around the room reluctantly rose as dubious and confused faces looked at one another. One man in the back spoke up on behalf of us all:

'Crime? Suicide isn't a crime.'

The professor took off her glasses and gently held them in one hand, gazing towards the man. 'You're right. So, why are we still saying that patients "commit" suicide?'

The silence was palpable. Some people were leaning forward, others were crossing their arms or legs in discomfort, due to the nature of the topic.

'We aren't in the business of convicting someone of the "sin" or "crime" of suicide,' explained the professor as she flicked through to her first slide. Individuals can complete suicide or die by suicide, but they certainly aren't a criminal or a sinner for doing so, which is what the use of the word 'commit' implies.

The professor's presentation made me think deeply about the ways we remember or talk about how someone died, and inspired me to consider all the conditions in which people will pass away and how we could remember and talk of each person's passing in a way that is respectful and beautiful.

The power of language

Our language has the power to determine the way our loved ones are remembered. Our language can bring us closer to healing and resolving our grief or drift us further away. When we use language that lends a kindness about our loved ones after they've passed, we create space for them to potentially interact and bless us with their presence. There is power in what we say because the first person to believe it is us. If we say our loved one 'lost their battle' with an illness, what do you think it might do to the way we remember that person at the moment of their passing? We can change the narrative on how we speak of loved ones simply by remembering the best versions of them.

When they decide to leave

I'd like to discuss suicide in a little more depth and how we can change the way we consider it, as someone who has spoken to thousands of spirits who have died in this way.

When we have to grapple with the reality that a person has chosen to end their own life, we can often face feelings of guilt about not being there at the right time or perhaps missing the cues or signs of their mental decline.

However, it's important to consider that beyond our reasoning or awareness, this person was struggling with something bigger than what we could imagine. For some, suicide is the end result of experiencing depression. It isn't 'giving up' or 'throwing in the towel'. For those who struggle immensely, in their darkest hours of depression, suicide can be a strong and rational thought.

On the other hand, I have met a long line of spirits who have said that they ended their lives due to many other reasons, such as messy break-ups, getting caught in an affair, being consumed by debt, fears they could never overcome, a family that forsook them, regrettable actions based on alcohol or drug taking – the list goes on. There are many reasons why people don't find their peace on Earth.

Whatever the circumstances, ultimately, to honour a spirit is to honour their choice – no matter how it affects you. It's not for you to try to measure or weigh up the rationality of their decision and consider whether, in your opinion, they could have muscled up and shouldered through their issues. Instead, this is a time to accept their choice completely and radically. Be assured that the conditions of their passing do not alter the conditions of their life, and know that the most enjoyable moments that they experienced are still relished and remembered – by them, but also by you. It's not how they died that we must remember, but how they lived.

I remember having a discussion with an old mate of mine who, like me, has quite a philosophical mind. He shared with me a sobering yet clear view of suicide that changed how I approached it. 'Consider life as a game,' he said. 'At any moment, you have a will to consider that you no longer want to play the game. It's as simple as that.'

This concept challenged me deeply, not because I had a job in mental health, specifically in the suicide prevention team at the time. It challenged my morals and my knee-jerk reaction to the heroism that drives us to pull people off hypothetical cliffs and save them from their perceived sorrows. My friend pointed out that most suicides are completed by people with rational minds and well-thought-out reasons.

In mental health we would call people like this, who have thought rationally about suicide, 'high risk' – particularly if they had been having these thoughts but not reached out for help or support. However, my friend had made me stop and think. Why should life automatically trump death? Who am I to superimpose my own values over someone else's decision? Though it might be a controversial opinion, I don't believe I have the right to do that to anyone. But it's a hard thing to grasp for those who believe in a person's right to have control over their own life, and yet find the loss of anyone they know by suicide to be understandably painful.

I'm by no means saying that nothing can be done to help someone who is thinking about ending their life. Help is always available to anyone who is experiencing suicidal ideation, or knows someone who is. My point is that once someone is gone, we need to accept that they didn't want to be in this world anymore, and there's nothing that we could or should have done that might have changed that.

One of my colleagues had a patient who was 84 years old and had made an attempt on her life. 'I want to be with my husband. I'm lonely, my kids are gone, my dog is gone, I have nobody,' was her rationale for wanting to depart. I recall that my colleague felt torn between their patient's stated desire to die and the reality that our medical system and even legal system are mandated to hold her feet here until she passes away by another means. This lady was strong and of sound mind, and explained to my colleague, 'I have lived a good life, an academic life, travelling the world, and it is my right to die when I want to.'

I know that many people go to mediums hoping to be put at ease about their loved one's suicide, with words such as, 'They miss you and they regret ending their life.' However, that's often simply not the case, which can be hard to accept. The reality is, when I contact the spirits of people who have suicided, they often tell me, 'I began to hate my life and I wanted to be with my spirit family.'

People who are really set on ending their life will find a way to do it, and often they will not regret it once they are in Spirit. It's a sad reality for some of us who continue to live on without them, but it's time to change the narrative and focus on their life and not *how* they passed. This is a complicated topic, but I strongly believe that to honour someone's passing, we should be honouring what we knew about them living.

No 'battles' exist

We've all at some point heard a variation on the phrase, 'They lost their battle with cancer.' What a terrible way of remembering someone who passed from cancer, to speak of them as if they had been defeated! Cancer is not something that you win or lose; it's not as simple as that. This figure of speech, and the whole narrative surrounding it, is something our society urgently needs to rethink.

The best way to honour someone who has passed from cancer or another serious illness is to not imply that they lost anything or fought with anything. Instead you could say something like, 'They didn't recover from cancer.'

Another term that people have adopted in speaking of someone's passing is to say that they have 'rejoined the spirit world'. This evokes positivity and allows the person's spirit to be honoured and to live on beyond their final moments. It highlights that they aren't experiencing ill health anymore and have been removed from the troublesome body that they laid in for a long time. This could apply to any bodily condition that a person will pass because of.

Remember that nobody wins or loses on their deathbed. Nobody is keeping score. You either heal and recover or you don't. And if you don't, you will still be cheered on (as mentioned in Chapter 10) for your bravery as you enter the spirit world.

Honouring with our actions

To honour a loved one's spirit is to celebrate their life, and the best way to do this is to simply remember their role in your own life. It's often a popular way to honour Spirit using actions because it is a soothing practice that helps us deal with grief uniquely. If they were your parent, sibling, partner or cousin, remember them as this person to you. Recall the moments where you would laugh yourselves into knots, the seasons in life that were the easiest for you both and you had each other's backs. There is so much beauty that we can focus on.

But how can we do this at the early stages of their passing or when it seems unbearable without them? There are ways you can actively honour the spirit of the one you dearly love and miss that they can be a part of, too.

Altars

A personal altar is a sacred space that you can set up in your home to pay homage to a soul who has departed. It is one of the most common and effective ways to honour a spirit for who they are today – as a being that has outlasted both their passing condition and their life shared with you – and to keep their memory alive. Altars can be set up on a small table and placed in a communal living space or hallway, or even placed in a special, dedicated room. On the altar, you can add items of importance and significance, such as jewellery your loved one owned or knick-knacks that they left to you. It can also be a beautiful thing to display photos of the person who passed, if you wish to, as well as candles and other special mementoes that could make the space special and sacred.

If the person was cremated, you could keep their ashes on the altar as their special place of remembrance and honour. You can also add any items that you feel connect you with the person – for example, feathers (see page 111), items that represent their passions and talents, their favourite perfume or cologne, etc.

There are no hard and fast rules when it comes to engaging with the altar. Some people spend a set moment every day (perhaps in the morning) kneeling at the altar and speaking to their loved ones as if they were in the room. Others only engage with it sporadically. The altar itself is simply a focal point to help you find a comfortable space and shift your awareness into honouring and linking in with your loved one.

Offerings

Some families like to take an offering to their loved one's resting place, or wherever their central point of remembrance is. An offering is a token of remembrance to the loved one.

It could be in the form of pouring their favourite beverage into the soil at their gravesite. Other offerings could be fruit, flowers, tobacco, a letter or poem, or anything else that you feel is something your loved one would appreciate. You can place the offerings at the gravesite or consider putting them on the altar you made for the loved one.

Tattoos

It's also quite common in Western cultures for people to get a tattoo in memory of a loved one. This is yet another way that you could honour their spirit. The tattoo itself is completely up to you – perhaps it could be a special saying on your wrist, or your loved one's spirit animal on your shoulder. It is common during psychic medium readings for tattoos to be brought up by Spirit to help the client realise that their loved one acknowledges this tattoo and appreciates what was done in memory of them. However, given the permanence of tattoos, this is of course a personal decision you should only make after much thought!

Songs

It's common at funerals to play songs that have great meaning, recall happy memories or were favoured by your loved one. People are sometimes split over this, though – for some, it's a great way to remember the person, while for others, it might be hard to ever listen to that particular song again. Some families who are musical or have strong ties to music will write a collective song for or about the loved one. This will then be beautifully performed or produced professionally so that this song can be played in memory of the person.

Music can be a deeply powerful way to remember your loved one, and can be used by Spirit to show that they are with you or visiting you – so if these songs seemingly play randomly on your playlist or on the radio, don't dismiss it as a coincidence.

Gardens

What better way to remember a loved one than to plant a special garden in their honour? It's common for schools, sporting teams or recreational clubs to plant a tree or have a memorial of flowers and plants for those members who have departed. Memorial gardens with a person's favourite flowers are always a positive and joyful expression of honour towards those we love and, especially when we might need a break from the world, to sit in the memorial garden made in memory of someone can feel like a warm hug.

Benches or chairs

Another common offering is to build or buy a seat and place it in a special location in memory of your loved one. This seat could also be placed alongside a tree that was planted in memory of the loved one or beside the altar at home. So, whenever you're missing your loved one, you can sit under the tree or on the seat and speak with the person honoured there. You can have these benches or chairs made by a carpenter and even engraved. These are keepsake pieces to which families can form a special, lasting connection.

These are simply some ideas and prompts that can take the guesswork out of deciding what to do if you feel you want to do something special for someone you miss. But there is no right or wrong way to honour those we love.

You can do as many of these things as you wish, but remember that it's a two-way street. Spirit wants to step closer into your space as well and provide you with support, even if you can't see it. In the next chapter, you'll find out how our loved ones step into roles that aid us in this life.

Three-minute exercise

Make a quick altar with something you have of your loved one at close reach. It could be a photo or even something they gifted you. Put it on a table or in a common space in your home and bless it by writing down one thing you'd like to honour about that person.

12

An invisible support

ONE WINTER A FEW years ago, I went on a hiking expedition with a group to explore the beautiful Maria Island off the coast of Tasmania. Maria Island is known as the Noah's Ark of Australia due to its abundant wildlife, which roams freely and fearlessly across the island. Because of the island's remote location, the leaders of the group went ahead a few weeks prior to our expedition and left boxes of fresh water along our hike to provide the hydration we would need along the way and so we wouldn't have to carry it along the route. We had to be fully self-sufficient with everything else, though – our hiking packs were chock-full of dry food, as well as clothing rolled up nice and tight so we could fit in all of the other necessities such as utensils and tools.

Early one afternoon, just as we were anticipating reaching the next water drop, our leader alerted us that we had made a wrong turn and were miles away from the correct spot. This was a rather horrifying discovery, as we had less than a dribble left in our bottles. We also needed the water to cook with that night, and any streams or other natural water sources were even further from us than the hoped-for water drop.

After much toing and froing, we decided to hike back in the right direction and finally reached the location where our leader believed the water had been left. We all set our backpacks aside to look desperately for the water, but the sun was setting and our window of time to complete the search in daylight was quickly closing. Our thirst was growing, along with our hunger.

As we continued frantically searching, the sun ducked behind the mountain, leaving us with the last of the light. Some hikers already had their torches out and the giggling and camaraderie of our usual hiking glee fizzled to subdued but palpable panic, heard through the rustling of our boots in the scrub. Hours passed.

However, instead of surrendering to fear and panic, I decided to turn to my guides and shoot up a quick prayer of request to show us the water we had been searching for. It was the only thing my reptilian brain could think to do before I was tempted to curl up in a heap of frustration and cry. Within moments of me finishing my inward and feeble prayer to my guides and ancestors, I felt compelled to look to my left and take two steps. Suddenly, a vague colour of blue was illuminated with the beam of my torch. As I stepped closer to it, I tripped over a rain-weathered box of water beneath my feet. I'd found it! My prayer had worked!

I shone my torch excitedly in a circle to find the other boxes of water, all sitting within a metre of each other. 'Guys, it's over here! The water is right here!' I shouted happily. The leader rushed towards me, relief etched all over his face, and I could hear the thumping of hiking boots as the rest of the group followed him through the gloom. Everyone hugged each other with joy and threw their hands up to high-five me for finding the water.

Later that night, we sat around the fire with our tents pointing towards each other in a circle. With our stomachs full and our mugs holding warm herbal tea, the leader asked how I was able to discover the water. Without any hesitation, I told the group that I had lifted a request to my guides and asked for divine help to show us how to find the water we so desperately needed. I knew there were atheists and non-spiritual people among the group, but after recounting my story I could see the curiosity on their faces and knew a little light had gone on inside their hearts. I knew my story of trust in my guides and ancestors had given them something to mull over as we trekked on in our expedition.

I could have easily stayed quiet and kept looking for the water without relying on anything but my torch and sheer determination. Would we have found it in time? I can't say. The catalyst that I, to this day, am fully convinced of was my willingness to turn to the invisible support that was watching us all along, that was above us in the trees, around us in the bushes, moving in and around us as we searched. This was nothing less than an incredible demonstration of the palpable support our spirit guides can have in our life. When we step back from our humanness and set aside our stubborn independence, we can be held by a support that is beyond what can be found tangibly.

What is a spirit guide?

A spirit guide is a being or figure in the spiritual realm that has assigned themselves to guide you in your journey here in the physical realm. Your spirit guide is usually the spirit of someone connected to you who has crossed over – a family member, a partner, a close friend, an ancestor, or even someone from a past life. A spirit guide is a helper.

Let's return to our sailboat analogy from earlier chapters. Just as your higher self is the rudder and Source is the wind inside the sails, your spirit guides are the rigging. They take cues from and capture the voracity and power of Source to create a system of support in your life.

A sailboat's rigging comprises a system of ropes, cables and chains, which support a sailboat's masts. The rigging is a comprehensive system that relies on small movements that interact and consequently participate in the working of the sailboat. Some spirit guides are prominent, such as the sails on a rigging system, and others are less obvious but still valuable, such as the beams of the rig or various pullies and levers. Each spirit guide plays their role in a collaborative way to ensure that you are supported

The most common thing that needs to be replaced, repaired or changed on a sailboat is the rigging system – it is usually updated or entirely changed every seven to ten years. In a similar way, your current team of spirit guides aren't always going to be the same ones you will have forever. I believe that Source and your higher self endeavour to whisk in new spirit supports and retire others whenever you move into new or distinctive seasons. For example, the spirit guide that walked you home from school each day is not going to be the same spirit guide that sits with you on a plane journey to visit your long-distance lover. As your life twists and turns, new spirit guides will weave in and out of your life as they see fit and will most likely completely renew every decade or so.

It's important to be aware that a spirit guide is not a deity or something that needs to be praised, worshipped or revered in the religious sense in order to guide you. A spirit guide is a loving being that is helping you out unconditionally.

Your spirit team

I believe there are many types of spirit guides but there are four in particular that are assigned to you at any given time.

The encourager

An encourager is a guide that will allocate itself to you at a moment in your life where you face interpersonal or private battles that involve an intensity of emotion, pain, trauma or stress. Your encourager guide knows what ticks you off – your triggers, your moods and tantrums, and everything about your emotional life. They are aware of the capacity of your mind and whether or not you have depressive or anxious thoughts often or irregularly. The encourager guide is purely responsible for lifting you up when you fall down. Like a coach to an athlete under pressure and stress in training, an encourager guide will cheer for you and always be on the side of moral support for you.

You will encounter your encourager guide subtly. For example, let's say you hit a depressive corridor in your life. You might be feeling hopeless and helpless about life, with sleep becoming worth its weight in gold, offering an escape from the drudgery of the daily grind. But perhaps at one point during this highly depressive time, you might feel a tiny urge to do the laundry that has piled up into a massive heap at the end of your unmade bed. You might not hang it out to dry for two days and perhaps will have to run it through another cycle, but hey, you got the washing into the machine. That's a great start!

The urge to tend to your dirty laundry is the inner voice of an encourager spirit guide.

It can be easy to simply ignore or dismiss the voice of the encourager. Perhaps it seems unreasonable to be so kind to ourselves when the thoughts running through our heads are harsh ones such as 'I've been so lazy', 'I haven't handed out enough resumés' or 'My debt is consuming me!'. Your encourager guide will flip things around and ensure that they bring in new patterns of thought that will help ease the stress and worry. It's up to us to acknowledge their guidance, let it sink deeply into our hearts and then act upon it.

The encourager guide often inspires the voices of others to interact with you, too. Perhaps you've been down on yourself or you've not given yourself enough credit for something. Your encourager spirit guide will open the mouth of someone to correct or inspire you. For example, I have an old friend who will often say something when I've been self-critical, beating myself up or being overly pessimistic about my actions or decisions. Instead of letting me get away with wallowing in my sorrow, I believe my encourager spirit guide has used this friend many times to literally say, 'Can you not speak about yourself that way, please, Cael? Please reframe that to be something of optimism and hope.' At times, your friends might not realise at all that they are being divinely used by spirit guides accessing their voices to help you recognise you're talking down on yourself and to provide encouraging words.

Your encourager guide could also use divine intervention through messages in books, magazines or advertisements. And they will never give up, until you receive the message. For example, you might be sitting at a barber or hair salon and feel the need to open up an old magazine that is the fourth one in the pile you've been given. As you flick open to a random page, the heading reads 'Self-love: Five ways to be kinder to yourself today'.

This is not a coincidence at all! The spirit guide who came along with you to your hair appointment is hovering in the space, analysing whether this brief moment while you're not being attended to could be used to speak to you. Perhaps they spent the morning trying to send encouraging Instagram posts to you but you swiped away before you noticed them. Now the spirit guide has cued a little notification in your mind to dig to the fourth magazine and open to page 28. With anticipation, they wait for you to realise that this was a divine message sent to you.

Encourager guides are there to do just that: encourage you with whatever resource or unique event they can arrange. It's like a covert mission for them to stay as unrecognised as possible but still encourage you without taking any of the credit. The best thing is, they don't require your belief in them or your acknowledgement. They serve by way of persistently trying to ensure you get their message.

The logistician

This might seem obvious, but your logistician is someone who is devoted to the logistics of your life. Perhaps in a past life they were your partner or in this life they took the position of your sibling. No matter their identity, the logistician is someone who is crossing the Ts and dotting the Is of your life. Think of them as the travel agent of your entire life.

Oftentimes you will have more than one logistician! They are cueing various opportunities into your life and analysing what steps will be needed to direct you forwards. Where your encourager guide is fully aware of every emotional whim you have, your logistician knows the layout of your day from start to end. They can predict precisely how you will react to certain things in your life. They know how fast or slow you move to act on even minor things. For example, they know how fast you like to pay your bills (or how slow, I should say, for some of you!). They are fully cognisant of how you spend your money and can see every last cent that you have to your name.

Your logistician is aware of every resource that you have. Do you know precisely how many cups of rice are left in your pantry? Or how many meals that can be made with the flour in your cupboard? Your logistician does! They are mathematical wizards and can calculate precisely how many meals, if need be, you could survive on with the items in your pantry if worst comes to worst.

Every property you own, every item of clothing, every sock that's missing – your logistician has weighed, studied, counted, analysed and checked off all of it. And that's only the beginning. Zoom out further and you'll learn that your logistician knows all the other resources you could possibly need, such as the last train out of the city at night, the closest Uber to you or the best rental to move you to for this time in your life.

Your logistician might seem like the most detail-obsessed spirit guide out of the bunch but aren't they handy! My logistician would have been immediately involved in the drama of the lost water on Maria Island and would have known before we even got within cooee of the water, exactly where it was waiting for us.

Out of all the types of spirit guide, a logistician is most likely to be the one you will never sense directly. You'll find it almost impossible to locate their 'fingerprint' on the ways they are guiding you. They are action-takers and thrive on organising and articulating in demonstrable ways how your life is trucking along. If you've ever worried about something in your life – really racked your brain over it, lost sleep over it and even had a meltdown in the living room over it – you can bet your spirit guide was watching from the sidelines. In fact, this one thing had probably been on their radar for months and they have exactly the right plan to steer you through it.

We humans often think a certain number of steps ahead in our lives, but the logistician has crafted a plan that goes much further. I wouldn't put it past the spirit world that they would, as a pack of logisticians, be having intense board meetings about everything that is up and coming in your life! Ultimately, the logistician is your eyes and ears and, if anything, it would prefer you let them do the worrying and you do the living part of your life.

The protector

Have you seen a bodyguard in action? They might just seem like a hunk of muscle on legs but they are an essential means of protection for the people they keep safe. In the same way that these people are protected, you are too – by your own dedicated unit of protector guides.

Perhaps you were involved in an accident from which you made a miraculous escape. Perhaps you were in the wrong place at the wrong time and were moved out of harm's way by a complete stranger. This is the work of your protector spirit guide, your defence system in the physical and spiritual realm. If it is in their power to do so, they will defend and protect you. It doesn't matter if you're the one who is putting yourself at risk in what you choose to do, your spirit guide will be walking beside you, ensuring you will find help.

Perhaps your spirit guide will prompt somebody else to be employed to assist. Think back to Chapter 7, where I talked about helping the two different intoxicated women off the street. It is highly likely that their spirit guides were aware of my request to Spirit about wanting to help more people, and employed me to assist.

Your protector is constantly measuring your safety in this ever-changing world of increased danger and uncertainty. The thing about our guides is that they never need sleep. They are always alert and can help us at a moment's notice.

Father figures often serve as protector guides but they can also be mothers. They act as an ongoing shield around you because you are their child. It comes as a natural response for many parents who have passed into the spirit world to then become the protector spirit guide to their children who remain in the physical world.

The manager

For some of us, our spirit teams themselves can be an elaborate system that needs organisation. This can be especially true for people in the public eye with high-profile jobs, or people with complex lives that need to be run efficiently behind the scenes. This is where the manager guide comes in. That being said, it's not a prerequisite to be a high-profile person to have one of these guides. I believe that we all have one in some capacity. A manager guide is there to assist you and your spirit team in using your 'god'-given gift to serve the world – and we all have one of those.

Similar to the way a talent manager organises their talent's speaking engagements, appearances and other miscellaneous logistics, a manager guide performs this role in our life from the spirit realm. The manager oversees the work of your spirit guides (aka your spirit team) in different aspects of your life. It's common for a manager guide to be one of the longest-standing spirit guides in your life.

Managers often present as serious and methodical. Unlike protectors, this spirit can remain somewhat aloof, as their connection to you is less emotional and more professional. For example, I have a manager guide who helps me in my mediumship at live shows or in my readings, but we are not very close. We have an interesting relationship – we trust each other completely, but I know she won't be wanting to linger after my shows!

She's a worker and manager in the sense that when I need to be 'on' for an audience, she's with me, but she doesn't hang out with me in my down time for the sake of it. If I'm doing a live session on TikTok, she's often standing a few feet away observing and cueing me when to do something or telling me when to wrap up. There's no messing around with her personality; I often describe her as a librarian, who I have a fondness for, but I would never want to bring my book back late or else!

How to meet your spirit guides

Now that you are familiar with the four main types of spirit guide, I'm sure you're wondering how you can connect in with them to better benefit from their services. Meeting your spirit guide is a relatively easy task – but I know for some people, the biggest barrier to connecting with their spirit guides is their own apprehension. Take three minutes now to consider the following steps.

Three-minute exercise

Take some deep breaths in through your nose and out through your mouth. Perhaps you could count your breaths – inhaling for a count of four, exhaling for a count of six. Allow your mind to find ease and stillness within this intentional, mindful breathing. Next, shift your awareness from your breathing to the present moment. What can you hear, smell and feel around you? Close your eyes and envision a small white light the size of a golf ball hovering inside your chest. As you focus on this light, picture it beginning to expand. With every exhale, allow this light to grow bigger until it envelops you in a sphere that continues to move outwards.

Once this white light has filled your whole room, imagine a purple light filtering in from the edges of the sphere. The white light in your chest represents your energy or frequency, and the purple light represents your spirit guide's energy. With every inhale, let the purple light move closer towards you. Once it is around two metres away from you, pause.

Ask the energy its name, then write it down. Ask its type and then write that down. Finally, make sure to thank it, because what you've invited closer to you is your spirit guide.

You can do this as many times as you want until you feel you've met all of your guides. Some spirit guides will come forward easily, others may not. This is because some aren't interested in being recognised or in directly engaging with you – they prefer to work at a distance. Utilising tools such as pendulums and oracle cards is also a great way to learn more about your spirit guides (more about these in Chapter 13).

Invisible and unconditional

The wonderful thing about spirit guides is that they don't require your input, belief or involvement with them to work. Unlike certain religions that are hands-on and transactional, requiring you to be practising some level of devoutness in order to receive support, your spirit guides will support you unconditionally, and remain switched on and engaged with your life here on Earth.

I have an old family friend that I grew up with. These days, she lives in Norway with her partner, and since we were teenagers, I've been linked in with her email newsletter that she set up for family and friends after she first announced she was going to Norway for what she initially thought would be a short trip. I would eagerly wait for her emails, in which she would share details with us about her travels in Norway and what she was doing. Lo and behold, while she was there she met the love of her life – and decided to stay for good! (Well, of course she's been back to Australia to visit, but Norway is her home now.)

The surprising thing is that, to this day, she has remained dedicated to pumping out content for this email newsletter. It arrives like clockwork, every six months, and has done so for a decade. She's shared it all: photos of her in the snow, news about finding a new job, stories about meeting her partner and moving into a new house, and even road-tripping through the Norwegian countryside. It's one of the most special newsletters that I receive and whenever I see her name pop up in my inbox, I smile.

What if someone was reading your newsletter of your life and smiling? Well, the fact is, Spirit is doing that right now. As your life progresses, updates are being logged in the spirit world through a wide chain of communication. Your loved ones are frequently tapping in to learn, see and experience your life in real-time in the other dimension. How is this possible? I have no clue! But I can certainly demonstrate – and do so all the time in my readings – the ongoing observations Spirit is making about us. So where it appears that your spirit guides are oblivious to your milestones, where it seems they don't have a clue what you're doing, I believe that they do! They 100 per cent know what's going on because they've signed up to your life newsletter! They want to cheer, smile and admire when new things arise in your life.

The interesting thing about spirit guides is that as mentioned, they are often our loved ones we so dearly remember who are operating as our invisible supports. But where did our loved ones go? And what about the spirits of those who aren't serving as guides? This chapter has shown you how to connect with your guides. Now it's time to find out how to reach everyone else.

13

Reaching Spirit

Now, MORE THAN EVER, people are wanting to find ways to interact with and communicate with the spirit world. The past few years have been rife with uncertainty, anxiety and loss, and have caused many people to look beyond the world around them for answers and reassurance.

The good news is, communicating with the spirit world is relatively easy to do. In this chapter, I want to share the best and most common ways for you to reach Spirit. (And for Spirit to reach you. Remember, it's a two-way street.)

How we can connect with Spirit

Here in the physical realm, in order to connect with loved ones, we need a method of communication – for example, Facebook, text messages, phone calls, email or a flight to their hometown. These tools allow us to communicate with those who are far away, and that same notion is good to consider when we are wanting to reach those in the spirit world. Let's explore the various tools and communication methods we can use to connect with Spirit both effectively and safely.

Before reaching out

When reaching out to Spirit, the first thing to do is to set an intention, and it's important that this intention is honest, genuine and sensible. This can be simply achieved by thinking about what you hope to receive from them – for example, an encouraging sign, or words of assurance. Try to resist calling upon spirits just to 'test' them, or because you're bored and in need of entertainment. If you truly want to reach them you can, but they won't appreciate having their time wasted!

Oracle cards

The most common way to communicate with Spirit is through the help of oracle cards. There are lots of different decks of oracle cards out there, including some that are made solely for the purpose of communicating with loved ones. But at the end of the day, it doesn't matter what kind of deck you use, as long as you have set your intention before you use them.

Ask Spirit to inspire you with a spread of cards, verbalising something into the open that you want some help on. For example, I often ask for a three-card spread from Spirit to convey a message to me regarding an important question I have about my life.

Next, begin to shuffle the deck of cards in a way that feels comfortable to you. There is no right or wrong way to do this. You can either wait until a card slips out of the pack or break the deck in half and select the card that lies in the middle. Repeat this twice more to end up with three cards in total.

Once you have your oracle cards, it's time to interpret the messages that you have received. Try to avoid only interpreting the card according to its corresponding explanation in the instruction book. Instead, stare at each card, one at a time, and determine a message from its imagery. In the psychic world we like to call this external clairvoyance.

It could be a message that appears abstractly in one of the cards. For example, as you stare at all the different aspects of the card's illustration, it may become apparent to you that an eagle's face looks determined. Perhaps you might then notice that the formation of the stars behind the eagle looks like the first letter of your first name. The message you've interpreted, then, could be that your spirit guide or loved one is rising you up like an eagle in the next step of your destiny. They want you to be determined and brave. Of course, this message may not be apparent in the booklet that comes with the deck, but it's something that you are understanding intuitively from your loved one.

When you practise this external clairvoyance, allow your mind to drift, and then take note of the first thing you consider upon finalising your shuffle. If you peruse the cards that fell or you selected and they all relate to the same theme – such as moving forward, healing, having courage or slowing down – then allow your mind to drift further to where you would place that theme in your current life. Oftentimes, by concentrating on one specific area, you help Spirit to then reply in a more specific, personalised way within the card spread.

For example, you might select a card with a dove, which you've always associated with 'freedom'. Thus the card is encouraging you to break free or to see how freedom relates to whatever you consulted the cards about.

Pay close attention to the nuances found in the card read. For example, you might notice that as you shuffle and a card falls out, it looks familiar to you – and then you realise it is the exact same tattoo pattern your loved one had. This would be an obvious sign or validation for you that they have been contacted and are inspiring each one of the cards to meet you with a message.

Issues to overcome with oracle cards

Every so often, you might not feel connected with the spread you've selected, or that the message is not making sense or aligning. At this point, you might want to consider some of the issues that can roadblock you from getting a clear reading:

- Your question is too specific and can't be answered in an oracle reading (see 'Pendulums' on page 175). To address this next time, ask a question that is a little more open-ended. Instead of 'Will I be pregnant in six months?', ask, 'What can you tell me about a pursuit of pregnancy?'

- You haven't set your oracle cards correctly at the commencement of the reading by calling upon the right person who you want to inspire the cards. To address this, next time, call upon your spirit guide to inspire the cards or a loved one who has passed.

- Your cards were given to you by someone else, or after purchasing them you didn't clear them spiritually with sage or some other cleansing energy to reset and reconfigure the energy to be channelled to you. In this case, smoke the cards with your favourite sage, palo santo or other cleansing substance, while saying something like, 'I clear these cards and reset them to my energy field.'

Automatic writing

Automatic writing is a practice whereby a spirit is believed to manipulate a person's pen to write a message or simply inspire the writer to communicate a message. This is the most common method that I use as a psychic medium – I often spend a few moments at the very beginning of a private reading using automatic writing to collate my information from the spirit world onto a blank page, to then communicate what is being said to the client.

Automatic writing is a tool that can link you in directly with your loved one, but there is a method you should use to be sure that you are correctly channelling your loved one. Before you begin writing, it's important to articulate a special intention into the spiritual realm so that your loved one is clear about what you're wanting to achieve by carrying out this practice. Start by asking a question that you want answered, or perhaps mentioning a topic you would like their input on. Write this topic or question at the top of the page for them to see. Here is a little script you might like to try to set your intention: 'Today I would like to connect with [insert loved one's name] and invite them to utilise the tool of automatic writing to answer my enquiry and communicate a message of hope to me.'

Once you have asked this, close your eyes and begin to swirl your pen in a corner of the page, allowing the ink to flow. Invite Spirit by focusing on the page and imagining that a white light is slowly moving towards the pen. Once you feel the white light has reached the pen, begin to write. It is very normal to feel at first as though it is just you who is writing. However, with the intention that you set and the visualisation task that you did, you will most likely have linked in directly with the person you need a message from.

Allow the inspiration to flow as the pen moves across the page, tuning in to any significant thoughts and feelings that you feel compelled to write down. When you feel a stop or pause, realise it's Spirit completing the answer or inspiring message. Take a breath and ask another question!

Just like riding a bike, automatic writing can take time to feel confident in. But with practice and consistency, it's very possible to reach a point where the pen will simply write with almost no effort from you. Even in the beginning stages, you will see a noticeable difference between your usual handwriting and the writing that appears on your page during a session of automatic writing.

Pendulums

Pendulums are great when you are looking for straightforward answers. But the flip side of this is that the response you receive will not be as richly detailed as an oracle card reading. And just like with any spiritual tool, it's important to set a clear intention for what you are hoping to achieve.

A pendulum can be purchased at any spiritual gift store or crystal shop or even made at home. It's important before using yours that you have cleared it of the energies that it has picked up on its journey to you. For example, if the pendulum was imported or purchased online, it will have been processed by many facilities in different countries and handled by numerous people. The energetic field of the pendulum will be static, just like the fuzzy screen on a TV when there is no signal. So before you use one you need to reset it and navigate to the right channel – your channel.

To do this, clear it by burning sage or palo santo or something you like, while saying some words over the pendulum such as, 'I clear the energy over this pendulum and claim it as mine. The energy surrounding it that has been picked up is now dismissed and I charge it with my own unique energy. I choose to use this pendulum for a good cause and with pure intentions.'

We must not only set our intention each time we use a pendulum, but we also need to clearly articulate the way we want to use it. For example, most people will ask their pendulum to swing backwards and forwards like a head nod if the answer to their question is 'yes'; to swing side to side like a shaking head if the answer is 'no'; and to swing around in a circle if the answer is 'I don't know' or 'maybe'. As I mentioned above, pendulums are great for letting your loved ones communicate straightforward 'yes' or 'no' answers, so be sure to keep this in mind when you're setting your intention and thinking of questions to ask.

Yes/no questions are an easy entry point for using pendulums. But you can also write down two different potential answers to your question – for example, two different universities you might someday want to attend – and let the pendulum swing towards one.

First, we need to set the pendulum and make contact. You could say, 'Today I want to utilise the help of my pendulum by communicating with [name the person]. If you answer the pendulum with "yes", please swing it back and forth; if it is "no", swing it side to side; and if your answer is "maybe" or "I don't know", simply swing the pendulum in a circle.'

Then we need to test whether contact has been made, which you can do by asking your pendulum questions to see if they will get it right. Start simple, with queries such as 'Is my name [your name]?' Wait for the pendulum to swing back and forth to say 'yes'. Next, ask a 'no' question, something like, 'Did I travel to France today?' Wait for the pendulum to swing side to side. Do this as many times as necessary until you feel convinced that the pendulum is actually alive. You have made contact with your loved one!

Now proceed with your yes/no question. Remember that it is all about intention and it doesn't matter how many questions you want to ask. Here are some examples of what you could find out from your loved one using the pendulum:

- Interpersonal questions, such as 'Am I being jealous?', 'Am I made for leadership?'
- Career advice, such as, 'Am I ready for the police

academy?', 'Should I pursue a career in makeup or hairdressing?'

- Love advice, such as, 'Is the second date worth a try?', 'Am I ready for love again?'
- Logistical advice, such as, 'Is this community right for my family?', 'Should I buy now or keep renting?'
- Career advice, such as, 'Is it the right time to request a pay rise?', 'Will I regret leaving my current job?'

As you can see, pendulums are a great way to get definitive answers and the tool is a wonderful means to get validation and evidence that you have connected in with Spirit.

Ouija boards

Ouija boards were invented in the late nineteenth century and became popular within the Spiritualist movement as a tool to connect in with spirits. They might instantly strike you as creepy, thanks to their reputation in popular culture, particularly horror movies. Perhaps you've always been told they're evil, don't go near them, you'll get possessed or the thing will be haunted. These are all just echoes of sensationalistic panic. If you set an intention that is genuine and serious, a Ouija board can be one of the most fulfilling ways to communicate with Spirit because you not only receive an answer but you get to have a tangible encounter with a spirit as it interacts with the board. Ouija boards are good for quick responses and engaging in a sustained dialogue with Spirit.

Of course, as with any spiritual tool, it's important to clear the board the moment you obtain it, cleansing from it any other earthly energies apart from your own. Or, better yet, you could try making your own Ouija board. You can find straightforward instructions online for how to do this.

Before you begin, don't forget to verbally state your intention of why you're utilising this tool and who you want to connect in with. If you have still a shred of uncertainty or nervousness, ask for a white light to surround you and for your spirit guides and ancestors to only permit through spirits of the light and of high vibration, and to disallow and seal the session from energies of low vibration. It's also good to ask to communicate with a particular spirit and then ask the spirit to spell out their name. If the name that the Ouija board spells out is not the name you want to contact, dismiss the spirit and start again, until your intended loved one spells out their name. It's best to hold a Ouija board session with someone else to amplify the high vibrational energy and usher in a spirit that you love faster.

Once you have happily used the Ouija board with good intentions and found your answers, close off the session by verbally disconnecting from the board. Say something like, 'I disconnect from the board and the spirit world, and thank my guides and loved ones for stepping forward.'

Mediumship

Going to a medium is a sure way to link in with Spirit. You can verbally and intimately experience Spirit sharing a message that they want to bring over and also answering questions for you in real-time. A mediumship appointment is a unique experience in which it's possible to find instant closure due to immediate contact with a loved one that shows that they are still existing and reachable elsewhere.

Preparing for a mediumship appointment requires you to set your intention. Consider why you want to see the medium, and work on calming your nerves beforehand. You will find that even through remote means, such as Zoom, a medium reading can still be accurate and helpful.

It's common practice, and can be a good idea, for people to seek a medium in pairs, such as siblings looking to communicate with a parent who has crossed over. That way if you get overwhelmed, you have someone else there who might be able to validate evidence or interpret something that Spirit is communicating.

In a mediumship appointment the psychic will communicate what they know about the spirit stepping forward – whether the person was male or female, what role they had in your life, how they passed away and other things such as what they're doing in spirit and who they have been reunited with in the spirit world. Memories that only you would remember are brought up, or specific things that can validate the person who is stepping forward. There are often times when more than one spirit who passed will come forward and share.

Issues with seeking mediums

Before you seek out a medium, it's always a good idea to consider whether it's the right time. Many people rush to a medium the moment someone dies because they believe it's what they need at that time. However, due to the grief a person experiences, their vibration will be naturally low and can put pressure on the session to the point where the spirit of the recently deceased may not come through. As a general rule, I find that it's best to seek a medium around six months after the passing.

If you can't connect to a specific spirit after several appointments with different mediums, don't be alarmed. Keep trying. When the spirit is ready, they will step forward.

Avoid mediums who ask too many questions. If they are truly a medium, they will not require much information and will be able to easily channel Spirit and provide validations about the person's personality, character, memories, etc.

How Spirit connects with us

Above, we've covered ways that we humans can reach out to those in the spirit world. But don't forget that your loved one can seek you out, too, to impart a message of their own. Here are some ways they might do that.

Telepathy

A common method that Spirit will choose to connect with us is telepathy – yet nine times out of ten we ignore it. Spirit will speak directly to us through our thoughts and feelings. You will simply know inside that when you're in need and you feel an answer or a gentle sense of encouragement floating towards you, it was Spirit.

Telepathic messages from Spirit are ever so subtle and non-threatening. Spirit will not interrupt you in aggressive ways or make unnecessary judgements over your life. If you hear something like that, it's probably not Spirit talking to you – it might be a shadowy part of your subconscious. Telepathy from Spirit will fall softly on the lens of your thoughts and often sound like your loved one communicating. For example, when my mother in spirit speaks to me, I can hear a lighter and feminine wave of thoughts come in that sound hopeful and encouraging, just as she always was. They are reasonable and often well timed.

During the height of the global pandemic in 2020, I recall lying in bed exhausted. I was losing hope and felt very miserable. To be honest, I flirted loosely with the idea of wanting to end my life but I knew this sense of despair was a collective and common theme among friends and the wider world because of how hope-draining this crisis was.

While lying in my bed with tears streaming down my face, I felt the presence of my mum in front of me. I heard her say beautiful and deeply logical things to me that dug me out of thinking so darkly. I can't remember exactly what she told me at the time but I knew it wasn't my own thoughts, as her sentiments had a strength and emotional maturity about them that opened my eyes to viewing things about my situation very deeply.

People

Spirit knows that if we don't pay attention to our own stream of thoughts and internal dialogue, we might heed the words of others. So, what better way for our loved ones to bring us a message than through those we interact with the most? As I mentioned in Chapter 12, often Spirit will use our loved ones in the physical world as vessels for delivering special messages from loved ones in the spiritual world. Although it doesn't necessarily use loved ones – even people that you don't particularly see eye to eye with can be utilised by Spirit to bring a message that can uplift you at a moment's notice. That includes strangers on the street or even the cashier at your local supermarket.

Nature

Spirit will often use visible things from the natural world to help alert us to their presence – for example, it's common for Spirit to send butterflies, feathers, dragonflies or various plants or flowers to show they are near. If you haven't received any of these little cues and messages from your loved one yet but would like to, it's simple to program these with Spirit. For example, say your loved one had a garden and would always admire ladybeetles. What you can say into the spirit world is something like this: 'Spirit, please show me ladybeetles to remind me that my loved one is watching over me and that I am on the right path.'

It won't take long before you start to see ladybeetles in odd places. Perhaps you'll be in a shopping centre and all of a sudden you go to sign your name on a receipt and the cashier hands you a ladybeetle pen. You head home on the train or bus and as you jump off, you see a teenager with a ladybeetle bag. They will start to pop up in so many ways!

This is one example of programming and setting an intention with Spirit to communicate with you in a specific way. For me personally, the cats I used to own were often the first sign my loved one was around. If I was feeling low and missed my mother, my old cat Rosie would come and jump on my lap. If I was experiencing anxiety or stress, my cat Louie would prefer to come and comfort me. Each cat somehow knew what supportive role they needed to play, showing that even our loved ones will use not only flora but fauna to reach us!

Numbers

Just like with Source and the higher self, you might start to see various patterns of numbers that indicate your loved one is nearby. For example, 44 could be the number you assign to your loved one because their birthday was 4 April. So now when you see 44 on a car's numberplate, or you are sitting at table 44 at a restaurant, these will be little reminders from Spirit that your loved one is around. It's fascinating, as often your loved ones will go out of their way to make sure that numbers in your life start to become a lot more attuned to whatever number is meaningful to you.

This is by no means an exhaustive list of signs or ways to communicate with Spirit. Spirit is finding ways to reach us all the time, and when we flick the switch and shift into a mental gear that acknowledges this, we will find a lot more comfort and hope. The biggest hope of all for us, though, is that there is no such thing in the universe as goodbye.

Three-minute exercise

Invest three minutes now in thinking of moments over this past fortnight when you might have been gently guided or reached a conclusion about something by way of intuition as opposed to cold hard facts. When did you follow your gut instinct?

14

There is no such thing as goodbye

ON THE DAY MY mother passed away, in the summer of 2014, I left school early. I was the first one home. I would have to wait for my family to return one by one to eventually mourn with them, but until then I had a few hours alone.

The moment I got home I jumped in the pool to cool off. I couldn't cry yet. Instead, I felt a strange peace around me. I had a confidence that Mum was okay and that she was around.

I remember, as I was bobbing up and down in the water, her voice coming through in my mind: 'There's no such thing as goodbye, my bub. I'm here.' This was the strongest and clearest message I have ever received from my mum. No other message has been able to permeate my heart like that.

My mum had always had an aversion to ever saying 'goodbye' or 'farewell'. Instead, she would say something along the lines of 'talk soon' or 'see you tomorrow' or even 'take care'. There was always the hope of seeing, speaking to or visiting her again, and I took great comfort in that – even after she had passed.

As a result, I have adopted this same message into the fabric of my relationships as an adult. I don't like to say 'goodbye' to people and I like to keep the number of people who I fall out of contact with at a minimum. Although my life is extremely busy and hectic, I try my best to show I'm still present and reachable.

Energy cannot be destroyed

We often view the passing of a loved one as the end and I know at times it can really feel like that. Many people consider their years-long marriage as having ended at the moment of their spouse's death, perhaps because of that famous line 'until death do us part'. But how strongly do you believe that love is stopped at the grave? I certainly do not think so. The number of husbands that come through, the number of wives, fiancé(e)s and true loves that step forward in my readings are too many to count. They bring up memories that nobody else but they and their partner would know. It's clear to me that they are still there.

Or what about your parent that raised you and supported you through all the ups and downs of life? Do they simply vanish into thin air? Absolutely not! This is the illusion of passing away. We think the person is unreachable or uncontactable, but that's just a perception. I have to say that I've probably met more dead people than I've met living! Why? Because they're all around us; they haven't gone very far at all.

The first law of thermodynamics (conservation of energy) states that energy is always conserved – it cannot be created or destroyed. In essence, energy will be converted from one form into another. It's never wasted in the universe. It is always being recycled to come back and make a new appearance in a different form. That means that anything in this universe has existed forever and will continue to exist beyond its observed 'end'.

The truth is, people pass away and within moments, they can be instantly contactable by spirit mediums. I've seen this with my own eyes.

It was a beautiful Saturday morning in the summer of 2020 and I was seeing my only client for the day. This lady had booked and paid for her session six months earlier due to my long waiting list. No special feelings, no fuzzy cues from the spirit world could prepare me for what would occur once I jumped on the video conference with her.

She was late. It was getting to six minutes past the hour

and I usually call a no-show at the ten-minute mark. The clock struck 10.06 am and a stressed woman joined the call, trying to get herself sorted in her dining room.

'I'm so sorry I'm late!' she said, catching her breath. 'I didn't want to cancel but my brother just died.'

My heart sank and my beaming smile and excitement flipped straight to shock and horror. 'Oh my god!' I said. 'I am so sorry. Let's reschedule, it's perfectly okay for us to rearrange this time so you can be with family.'

'No, no, I've been waiting six months, I am so ready for this appointment now,' she replied without hesitation. She wiped her tears away and tried to compose herself while obviously checking her phone, waiting for updates to come in in real-time.

Instantly, her grandmother stepped forward in the spirit realm and started off the reading, bringing comfort to the woman and sharing with me that she had passed eight years prior. Then, all of a sudden, a gentleman started to appear to my left, slowly moving closer.

I stopped and said, 'He's here! Your brother was brought here to the reading by your ancestors.'

I described the brother to my client: a burly man who was simply a teddy bear underneath. Devoted to his friends all his life. He had no special career or outstanding achievements but was seen as a bridge between members of the family by simply being his unique self.

'They were just down at the river having fish and

chips – he had a heart attack and family are literally at the hospital right now,' I explained to the client, passing along what he was communicating to me. As far as she knew of the events at that moment, I was correct.

It was remarkable: I was directly watching as a woman learned of her brother's passing but she was in my presence, as a medium holding a connection with her brother in real-time. The reading was cut short as she was called to travel to the hospital but she thanked me for this reading that had turned out to be perfectly timed. Even a few hours later, she would not have had the special moment that brought comfort to her in the exact moment her brother had passed away.

This is a unique story. This is not a regular weekly event for me, nor even something that might happen in a whole year. What it taught me is that the moment someone passes, their spirit is continuing to live on. Spirit is not in some sort of holding bay, as certain theories suggest; they don't need to be left for 40 days before they can be contacted. They can even find their way to a medium session that their sister booked without their knowledge to originally speak to her grandmother, never intending to speak to someone she assumed would be alive at the time of the reading.

I do want to mention a caveat here, which is that I prefer for people to wait until six months have passed before connecting to Spirit. As I have stated above, this is not because I believe that the spirit needs time to settle and find its way. The truth is that we need to grieve. When we are hit by shock and grief, our vibration naturally dips. A low-energy vibration is not ideal for a psychic reading and at times can make a connection completely impossible. That's why I advise my clients to wait six months until the initial shock has generally passed.

But what about the woman and her brother? Well, in this case she had not even had time to feel shock or let grief soak in. Everything was so fresh and there was some peace or safety from being in my presence as a medium that left her feeling hopeful and her vibration lifted. This resulted in the connection with her brother in spirit right away. Now this will always be something she remembers when she considers her brother: her grief began with a message that he was okay, that he had only passed moments prior to the appointment but he had already found their grandma and was instantly at peace.

Even for the rest of us who don't experience something this rare, like my client did, the lesson is that our loved ones continue on in energetic form as soon as they leave their physical bodies, and they are able to instantly find peace and communicate with us through willing vessels if they wish to.

Let go of guilt

I find it sad that some people become crippled by the feeling that when their loved one passes, that's it – they will never see, hug, talk to or know them again and there is no chance to put anything right. I'm convinced that this isn't true; we *will* see our loved ones again. This hope can help us move on from the grief and guilt we can face about people's passings. This is because we have the faith that we will be reunited again with them and once more hear that they love and accept us.

Perhaps you had an argument right before they passed, or you promised you would be there for them but you couldn't make it. Any number of practical issues may have led to you not being able to tell them you loved them one last time or to share a special moment with them before they passed. Death is complicated, and even more so the actual time of passing. Nothing and nobody can prepare us for it.

I want to emphasise to you that if you did miss your loved one's passing or even chose to not be there for a range of reasons, it's okay. It happens all the time – sometimes people are sick, far away, or perhaps they have simply decided that being there would be too overwhelming. These kinds of guilts can haunt us for years, or even decades, but it really shouldn't. I've given readings to many who have been in this position.

One story that stands out in my memory is about a father in spirit who told his daughter that it was not her fault that she could not make it to the hospital before he died, because she could not have saved him. The daughter in question was pregnant and stuck at home with her other child, and her relief when I communicated her father's words to her was palpable. It was a weight off her shoulders.

Be brave

I find that now more than ever before, people are looking for comfort or even just a 'hello' from their loved ones who have crossed over. What used to be a practice that was frowned upon by religion has shifted. I'm seeing lots of Christians and Muslims who understand that what mediumship is achieving is something God, Source or the universe is directly behind. They understand that no malevolent force is engineering the work of mediumship. Why would it? Mediumship is producing hope in people. And why would malevolence want hope?

I believe that more and more people will rise up and embrace their intuitive gifts. My ultimate hope is that we will all realise that we can move closer to Spirit and we don't need to be afraid. We can leave behind the old ways of thinking that make us scared, worried or guilty about seeking out spirit mediums.

If we are to truly embrace the notion that there's no such thing as goodbye, we must take the bold and brave steps to say 'hello again' to our loved ones. The first step to doing this is simply acknowledging Spirit's ongoing existence and shifting our awareness to realise that they are present, whether we believe or accept it or not.

Given that the nature of being is an energy form, we won't ever vanish and nor will our loved ones, spirit guides or Source. All of this is too precious for it to just disappear and be forgotten. This is an encouraging and hopeful thing to remember. Many cultures around the world acknowledge this and hold 'celebration-of-life' parties. Instead of wakes (which, in my experience, are depressing and sad and filled with people nibbling sheepishly on finger food and sipping on coffees, feeling lost), a celebration-of-life party is an opportunity for a family to acknowledge that a person's life was completely worthwhile. In their minds they know that this isn't a farewell party or goodbye but a 'see you soon' to their loved one, which helps people to deal with grief and loss.

I've quizzed many of my friends and people closest to me about what their hopes are, and one of the greatest is always to see their loved ones again when they cross over. Buried deep in the fabric of all of us is the knowledge that we will again be reunited with our loved ones. Our spirits are aware of the fact that our higher selves are beyond us in a wider web of connection.

If your life was a sailboat, with your higher self as the rudder, your spirit guides the rigging and Source as the wind in your sails, then Spirit is the ocean. An ocean that outlasts centuries with poise and determination. An ocean that carries your boat on its surface no matter how heavy it may get.

Have you ever heard the phrase 'their spirit is bigger than life'? That is precisely it: our spirit is like the ocean, it is bigger than this life. Our spirit is bigger than addiction, loss, trouble, debt, fear or overwhelm. We have a network, a tribe, a nation behind us in the spirit world that stands up for us when we can't stand up for ourselves. We have eyes watching and hearts cheering from beyond us to support us when we can't help but break down. There is no need to say goodbye because Spirit never actually leaves.

No matter how you look at it, we don't have to search very far. We don't even have to try very hard. Behind and before us we are held by Spirit; above, within and beyond.

Three-minute exercise

Record a three-minute voice note to your loved one, updating them about your life right now. Listen to it over once.

If you can, set a reminder in 60 days to listen to the voice note again and hear how you spoke of your life 60 days ago. Has anything changed? Finally, realise that your loved one has never needed the voice note. This is how good they are at keeping up to date with you.

Resources

If anything in this book has raised any issues for you, please don't hesitate to contact the following organisations.

1800RESPECT
1800respect.org.au
1800 737 732

1800RESPECT provides confidential information, counselling and support service for people experiencing sexual, domestic and family violence.

Beyond Blue

beyondblue.org.au

1300 22 4636

Beyond Blue provides trusted resources and a support service for anxiety and depression.

Lifeline Australia

lifeline.org.au

13 11 14

Lifeline provides access to 24-hour crisis support and suicide prevention services for all Australians who are experiencing a personal crisis.

QLife

qlife.org.au

1800 184 527

QLife provides anonymous and free LGBTI+ peer support and referral for people in Australia wanting to talk about sexuality, identity, gender, bodies, feelings or relationships.

Suicide Call Back Service

suicidecallbackservice.org.au

1300 659 467

Suicide Call Back Service is an Australia-wide service that provides professional 24-hour, seven-day-a-week telephone and online counselling to people who are affected by suicide. You can get immediate help via phone, webchat or video chat.

Acknowledgements

I want to start by acknowledging my ancestors and spirit guides that inspired and helped me with this book. I appreciate firstly my mother in spirit for helping me with ideas but also keeping me company on lonely nights trying to meet deadlines. I thank spirit guides Acey, Michael and Lao for opening up the doors and possibilities for my book also to manifest into this dimension.

I want to thank Isabelle, my amazing publisher, who saw what *Three Minutes with Spirit* could be and allowed my voice to translate to the public. I appreciate you finding me and allowing me to create my first body of work.

I want to thank Genevieve, my helpful editor, for her saint-like patience in working with me and my often-busy schedule. I appreciate how you always gave me clear guidance and solid feedback in this unknown terrain of authorship.

Finally, I thank my manager, Angylina, for holding the fort for me on days when I had to literally bunker down in my own home to write. Thank you for supporting me on all fronts, even when things seemed so unfamiliar. (Funny story – at one point, Angylina confiscated my phone so we had to communicate through Gmail chat. It felt like the old MSN Messenger days, for those who remember it.)

About the author

Cael O'Donnell is one of Australia's most highly sought-after psychic mediums. His childhood in country Victoria was full of challenges and inspired his professional career as a mental health therapist, helping people at their lowest points find hope to live. When Cael began sharing messages of healing and connection on TikTok, it helped him rediscover his lifelong passion for spirituality and led him down a new path as a psychic medium. He now has more than half a million followers online, has a 6–12-month waiting list for appointments, and has distilled his practical advice on becoming more spiritually grounded in his first book, *Three Minutes with Spirit*.

Discover a
new favourite

Visit **penguin.com.au/readmore**